SOUTHERN CROSSINGS

GOURMET TRAVELLER

AUSTRALIA

INSPIRED ESCAPES + CULINARY JOURNEYS

ACKNOWLEDGEMENT OF COUNTRY

Gourmet Traveller and Southern Crossings acknowledge all Australian Aboriginal and Torres Strait Islander peoples of this nation as the traditional owners of the lands featured in this book. We also acknowledge the Gadigal people of the Eora Nation, as the custodians of the place we now call Sydney, where this book was edited and published. We pay our respects to ancestors and Elders, past and present. *Gourmet Traveller* and Southern Crossings are committed to honouring Australian Aboriginal and Torres Strait Islander peoples' unique cultural and spiritual relationship to the land, water and seas and their rich contribution to society.

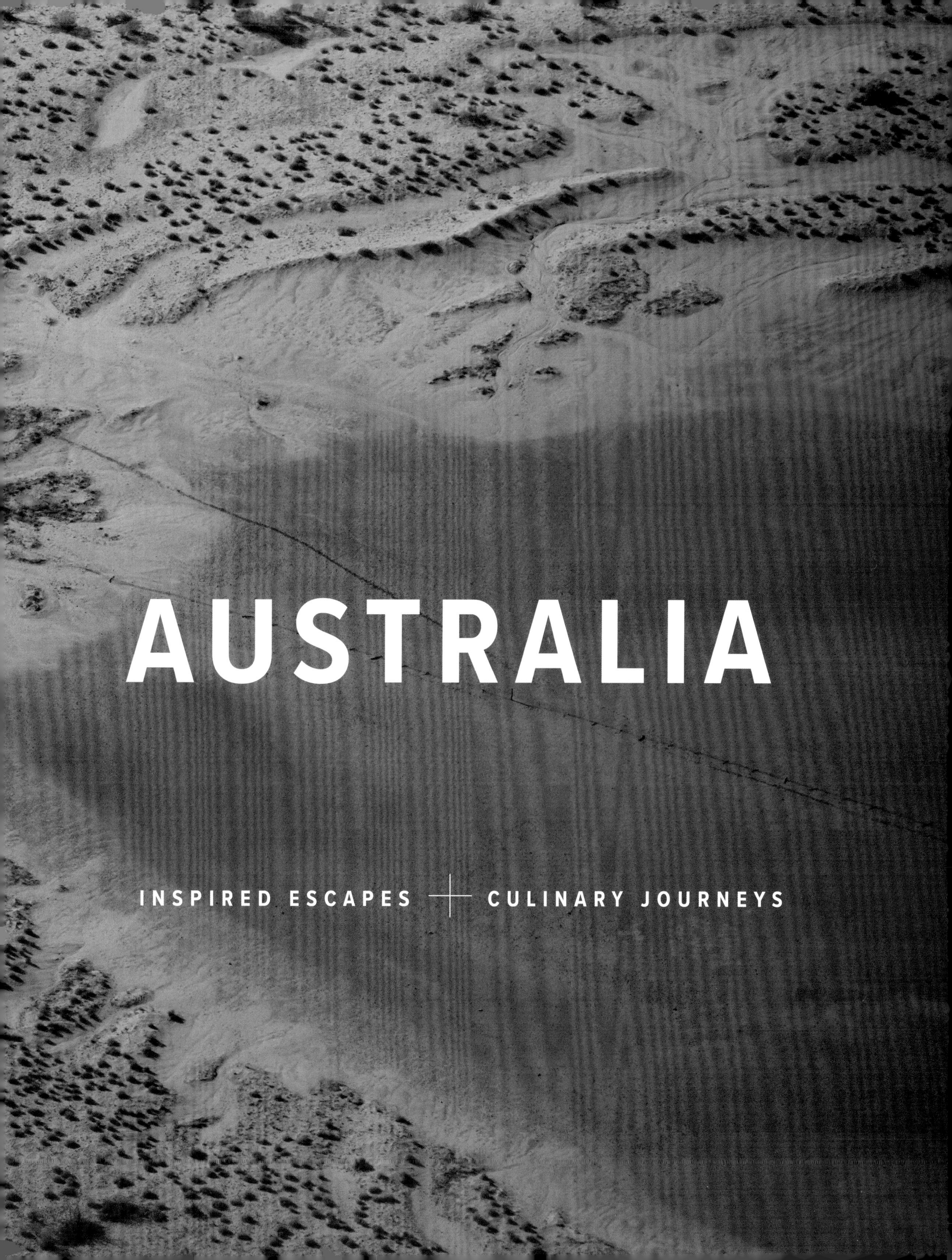

AUSTRALIA

INSPIRED ESCAPES + CULINARY JOURNEYS

By the coast

Among the trees

CONTENTS

Under big skies

In the vines

GREAT SOUTHERN LAND

We love our sunburnt country. Australia's natural beauty with its diverse terrain and unique places to stay, make it the perfect destination for local and global travellers alike. What's most exciting is the endless variety of adventures our great southern land offers. From the iconic red earth of Uluru-Kata Tjuta to the sprawling Tasmanian wilderness and the tropical islands of the Great Barrier Reef, Australia's diverse splendour is the constant source of both inspiration and celebration at *Gourmet Traveller*. It's that splendour that has led us here, to our first travel cookbook, presented in partnership with Southern Crossings.

In these pages, we take you on a culinary journey, as we explore some of the country's most luxurious properties and resorts, and ask their chefs to share recipes that offer a taste of their unique landscape. While each of these luxury retreats is different, their kitchens share a common commitment to fresh, seasonal and local ingredients. Seafood dishes include Moreton Bay bugs at Jackalope, Freycinet Marine Farm black mussels at Saffire Freycinet and Pemberton marron at Cape Lodge. Native ingredients feature in recipes with karkalla at Longitude 131° and saltbush leaves at Spicers Peak Lodge. Whether you're after a rejuvenating wellness escape in the Byron Bay hinterland, an indulgent Whitsundays retreat or an invigorating outback adventure, a uniquely Australian experience awaits. We love exploring our great southern land, through both travel and food, and we hope these recipes and landscapes will bring you a taste of Australia and inspire new adventures to come.

Southern Crossings pioneered the concept of bespoke luxury travel in the Antipodes in 1986 with its vision to "enrich and inspire by creating extraordinary journeys". The dramatic landscapes of Australia, New Zealand and the islands of the South Pacific were the perfect canvas to create personally curated luxury travel designed for the most discerning of travellers.

More than three decades later, Southern Crossings continues to lead the way in tailor-made vacations and ultra-luxe travel experiences in the southern hemisphere. While the definition of luxury travel has evolved over the years, Southern Crossings' commitment to delivering luxury travel experiences with unparalleled service has not. Today's discerning travellers want more than just luxury; they seek authentic, personal travel experiences that offer a chance to connect with, and positively impact, the people and places they visit.

Every Southern Crossings' travel experience starts with a blank canvas and is designed for the individual client, reflecting the tailored approach that makes this company the leading luxury travel specialist in Australia. Each itinerary incorporates the combined knowledge, perspectives and connections of the company's travel design team to create bespoke luxury travel experiences that exceed the highest expectations.

Discerning and discreet, Southern Crossings has earned its reputation as an industry leader and Australia's trusted travel expert with a loyal client following and numerous prestigious industry affiliations.

Southern Crossings' owners and directors, Stuart Rigg and New Zealand-based Sarah Farag, are both well known for their travel expertise with a slew of awards for their contribution to the industry. For more than 35 years, the company has shared its expertise, insider knowledge and secrets

to curate memorable luxury travel experiences for discerning international travellers in Australia, New Zealand and the islands of the South Pacific.

The Southern Crossings travel design team now also shares its experience and insights as well as its connections and long-standing industry relationships to inspire and delight sophisticated Australian travellers.

With a well-travelled clientele that includes foodies and families, honeymooners and lovers of all the very finest things in life, Southern Crossings' mission is always clear: to deliver unparalleled personalised luxury travel experiences that feed your passions and match you with your perfect place and pace.

Culinary experiences are often at the heart of Southern Crossings' bespoke luxury experiences and the recipes from each of the properties in this book are a testament to the power of food to transport you to another place. Food can inspire

curiosity, flavour your journey, and evoke travel memories to be savoured and shared. With this in mind, Southern Crossings has created uniquely Australian culinary-focused luxury travel experiences to take you behind the scenes. Whether you choose to dine under the stars in the outback or in the treetops in the Daintree Rainforest, you'll discover a world of flavours to match the unique destination.

Through culinary connections that go beyond the familiar tourist trail, Southern Crossings introduces travellers to award-winning chefs and winemakers as well as the talented local producers and providores behind some of Australia's best-kept culinary secrets. From bush tucker to fine dining, every corner of the continent offers a different taste of Australia. And that is what Southern Crossings delivers in one-of-a-kind culinary journeys.
southern-crossings.com

BY THE COAST

With pristine sandy beaches and turquoise waters, a tropical oasis awaits off New South Wales' northern coast and Queensland's Great Barrier Reef. Or try a different kind of coastal escape in the tranquil waters of Tasmania's Freycinet Peninsula or cruising the Kimberley coast. One thing's for sure, you've never tasted seafood this fresh before.

Halcyon House

This '60s surf motel at Cabarita Beach has been gloriously refurbished into a boutique beachfront hotel that exudes laidback luxury and offers one of the best hotel restaurants in the country.

Transformed into a luxury oasis with a Hamptons-meets-Mediterranean vibe in a calm blue-and-white palette, this former surf motel is the perfect place to soak in the serenity of New South Wales' Tweed Coast. Located on the pristine white sands of Cabarita Beach, guests can spend halcyon days by the pool sipping signature cocktails, dine at its award-winning restaurant or relax at its decadent spa.

When sisters Siobhan and Elisha Bickle bought the '60s surf motel in 2011 they wanted to create an idyllic holiday house for families to share. "We wanted [Halcyon House] to give guests the opportunity to recall past memories of their favourite beachside holidays," says Elisha.

Opening in 2015, Halcyon House took two years of planning and 15 months to build. The renovations were led by Sydney architect Virginia Kerridge, while the rooms were designed by Brisbane interior designer Anna Spiro.

Each of the 21 rooms showcases Spiro's signature eclectic style with fabric-upholstered walls, bold colour, exuberant patterns and quirky retro details with antique furniture, king beds and a private balcony or terrace. Many of the vintage pieces and furnishings, such as John Derian sofas, Madeline Weinrib rugs and drawings by Wayne Pate, were personally sourced by Spiro.

"I love visiting each room, looking at the various antiques and one-of-a-kind furnishings. I have many wonderful and funny memories behind how we came across them," says Elisha.

Halcyon's award-winning restaurant Paper Daisy focuses on using local regional produce and sustainably sourced seafood to deliver a truly memorable dining experience. Apart from its sensational breakfast offering (it won Best Breakfast at the GT Hotel Awards in 2018), Paper Daisy offers a stellar list of poolside snacks as well as an inspired à la carte menu. Halcyon House gin bar is home to one of the largest selections of Australian gins in the country with more than 120 gins from 40 distilleries.

The tranquil Halcyon Spa designed by Spiro in soothing green, timber, white marble and Moroccan mosaics is the ideal space for guests to enjoy restorative Sodashi facial therapies and pampering massage treatments. The two-storey retreat has four treatment rooms as well as a bespoke steam room and relaxation lounge area.

For those looking to explore the area, follow the coast north on one of Halcyon's complimentary bikes, hike Norrie's Head to watch the sun set, meet local producers at Mullumbimby Farmers' Markets or visit Husk Distillers, whose Ink Gin stars in Halcyon's signature cocktail.

EXPLORE

• Jump on one of Halcyon's complimentary bikes and follow the coastal path to Kingscliff where you'll find a choice of places to eat and rest after your ride.

• Relax and rejuvenate at Halcyon Spa with a menu of restorative holistic treatments designed to pamper body and soul.

Coal-roasted red cabbage, beetroot, Davidson's plum, lentils and native thyme

SERVES 6 // PREP TIME 45 MINS // COOK 3 HRS

"Cooking over fire is traditionally reserved for meat and seafood but giving vegetables the same treatment over coals pays," says executive chef Jason Barratt. "The earthiness of beetroot ties in with the minty sharpness of native thyme and Davidson's plum."

1.6 kg small red cabbage
1 kg beetroot
250 ml red wine vinegar
1 tbsp honey
100 gm frozen Davidson's plums (see note), thawed, or small blood plums, cut into small pieces
Dried crushed pepperberry, to taste (see note)
Native thyme, to garnish (see note)

BRAISED LENTILS
2 tbsp extra-virgin olive oil
1 carrot, finely chopped
1 onion, finely chopped
1 large celery stalk, finely chopped
100 gm Persian red lentils or green lentils (see note)
500 ml boiling water
500 ml vegetable stock, boiling

CASHEW CREAM
150 gm roasted cashews
250 ml boiling water

1 Place cabbage over a charcoal fire, rotating, every now and then, or until the cabbage is soft to touch (3 hours). Take care not to burn the cabbage. Alternatively preheat oven to 100°C. Place cabbage on an oven tray lined with baking paper and roast until soft (3 hours).

2 Peel then thinly slice 1 beetroot. Combine vinegar and honey in a small bowl. Add sliced beetroot; toss to combine. Refrigerate until required.

3 Pass remaining beetroot through a juicer. You will need 250ml juice. Simmer beetroot juice in a small saucepan over medium heat until juice is reduced by half (15 minutes) then stir in the Davidson's plum pieces and season to taste.

4 For braised lentils, heat olive oil in a frying pan over medium heat. Add carrot, onion and celery; cook, stirring until vegetables begin to soften (5 minutes). Stir in lentils, then gradually add combined boiling water and stock, a ladleful at a time, stirring between each addition until liquids are absorbed and lentils are tender (30 minutes). Season with salt and pepperberry.

5 Meanwhile, for cashew cream, place cashews and boiling water in a high-speed blender and blend for a few minutes until smooth. Season to taste.

6 To serve, slice the red cabbage into sixths, fill between leaves with cashew cream and drained pickled beetroot slices. Place cabbage on top of the braised lentils and serve with the Davidson's plum and beetroot sauce. Garnish with native thyme.

NOTE Davidson's plums, pepperberry and native thyme are available online from native-food specialist stores. The Persian red lentils we use are unsplit, reddish brown and hold their shape. Don't be tempted to use split red lentils as these will collapse.

PREPARE AHEAD Cashew cream and pickled beetroot can be made a day ahead.

WINE MATCH 2019 Brokenwood Indigo Vineyard Pinot Noir, Beechworth, Vic.

Sour tomato cappelletti, stracciatella, zucchini and marigold petals

SERVES 6-8 // PREP TIME 2 HRS (PLUS 4 DAYS + 2 HRS STANDING) // COOK 8 HRS 15 MINS

"This cappelletti is always popular with our guests," says Barratt. "Fermenting tomatoes gives the dish a freshness, similar to how freshly squeezed lemon lifts seafood. You need to ferment the tomatoes days ahead to intensify the flavours, but it's worth it."

Extra-virgin olive oil, for drizzling
Marigold petals, to garnish

SOUR TOMATO PASTE (SEE NOTE)
400 gm vine-ripened tomatoes, chopped
1½ tsp fine sea salt

FILLING
250 gm stracciatella (see note)
60 gm finely grated parmesan
100 gm fresh ricotta
1 egg

PASTA DOUGH
365 gm "00" flour
4 large eggs, at room temperature
1 tbsp sour tomato paste
Pinch of salt

PICKLED ZUCCHINI
2 tbsp water
1 tbsp caster sugar
50 ml white wine vinegar
½ tsp fennel seeds
1 zucchini, thinly sliced lengthways

1 For sour tomato paste, three days ahead, combine tomatoes and salt in a bowl, cover with a clean tea towel and set aside at room temperature for 48 hours to sour. Strain mixture through a sieve lined with cheesecloth, then gather the cloth and suspend over the bowl leaving it to drain further (1 hour). Reserve and refrigerate drained tomato water to serve. Spread tomato solids over a dehydrator tray lined with baking paper. Dehydrate at 45°C until jammy (8 hours). Process dehydrated tomato in a food processor to a paste. Refrigerate until required.

2 To start filling, one day ahead of serving, drain stracciatella in a sieve over a bowl and reserve drained milk to serve.

3 For pasta dough, on day of serving, pulse ingredients and a pinch of salt in a food processor until a rough dough forms. Turn out onto a lightly floured surface and knead until smooth (5 minutes). Wrap in plastic wrap and rest in the fridge (1 hour).

4 Meanwhile, for pickled zucchini, stir water, sugar, vinegar and fennel seeds in a saucepan over medium heat until sugar dissolves and mixture boils. Pour over zucchini in a heatproof bowl and leave to cool. Refrigerate until required.

5 To laminate pasta, divide dough into 3 equal pieces, then, working with one piece at a time and covering remaining dough with a damp tea towel, flatten it with a rolling pin or the palm of your hand. Dust lightly with extra flour and gently feed it through the pasta machine, starting at the widest setting.

6 Fold the two ends of the dough towards each other, then rotate dough 90 degrees and feed through the pasta machine again. Laminate once or twice on the widest setting, then continue to feed dough through the machine, reducing settings, notch by notch, until the pasta is 1mm thick. Repeat process with remaining dough, then fold and place in a single layer on a tray dusted with extra flour. Cover until ready to use.

7 To finish filling, mix drained stracciatella, parmesan, ricotta and egg together in a bowl. Season to taste with salt and white pepper.

8 Using a cutter, cut out 8cm rounds from pasta sheets (discard scraps). Place rounds in a single layer on a tray dusted with extra flour.

9 To make cappelletti, spoon filling into a piping bag fitted with a 2cm nozzle. Pipe 10gm filling onto the centre of each round. Working with one pasta round at a time, lightly brush edge with water, fold over to enclose and form a half moon shape. Press edges to seal, expelling all air. Holding the half-moon in both hands, fold the top of the rounded side in towards you, while bringing the corners together; slightly overlap the corners and pinch them to seal to form a little round "bonnet" or "hat" shape. Place on the floured tray. Repeat with remaining pasta rounds and filling. Makes 35.

10 To cook cappelletti, bring a large saucepan of salted water to the boil. Add pasta, in batches, and return to the boil, stirring gently, until pasta is cooked (3 minutes). Drain.

11 To serve, divide cappelletti and drained pickled zucchini among bowls. Drizzle with stracciatella milk, sour tomato water and olive oil. Garnish with marigold petals.

NOTE If short on time, substitute tomato paste for sour tomato paste. Stracciatella is available from select cheese shops. If it's unavailable, substitute burrata or mozzarella.

PREPARE AHEAD Pasta can be made ahead and frozen. Cook from frozen.

WINE MATCH 2021 Dominique Portet Fontaine Rosé, Yarra Valley, Vic.

Capella Lodge

If you're looking for pure escapism, Capella Lodge on World Heritage-listed Lord Howe Island, offers an off-the-radar luxury retreat with first-rate dining and unparalleled views.

Resting 600 kilometres off the east coast of Australia, Lord Howe Island is well and truly off the radar. Accessed by a two-hour flight from Sydney, this subtropical paradise is characterised by white sandy beaches, crystal-clear blue waters and impressive volcanic peaks.

Capella Lodge sits at the southern end of the island, overlooking a vast expanse of ocean and the green peaks of Mt Gower and Mt Lidgbird. The luxury beach-house style retreat is set among lush palms and frangipani trees, with hidden beaches and picturesque walks just a stone's throw from your suite. Days on Lord Howe Island are the kind that you hope will never end, hiking along rainforest tracks, swimming in turquoise waters and exploring the world's southern-most coral reef.

With such seclusion and beauty comes a culinary experience to match. Capella Lodge's dining is at once refined and generous, international and island-inspired. Capella's chefs bring a clean, light style to the daily changing menu, designed to champion abundant local produce; fresh fish, local fruit and vegetables and even sea succulents and coastal flora foraged from the island.

Lunch can be enjoyed over a long afternoon in the sunshine at Capella's restaurant or alternatively as part of an island adventure. Curated barbecue and picnic provisions are easily packed away into a backpack for you to enjoy on a walk, at the beach, on a kayak or at one of the island's many idyllic picnic spots.

As Lord Howe locals, the chefs are passionate about their UNESCO World Heritage-listed home and the rich harvest that springs from its fertile soils and bountiful waters. In their spare time, they can often be found fishing for trevally, Lord Howe kingfish or yellowfin tuna, or foraging along the coastline. Sunset drinks and canapés cap off the day as the sun slips behind a pink-hued horizon and segues easily to dinner. While locally caught kingfish and tuna carpaccio remain popular, if you're looking to sink your teeth into something a little more substantial free-range meat from New South Wales features on the menu as do island-grown greens and house-made bread and pasta.

Set in a location as incredible as Lord Howe Island, Capella's relaxed aesthetic lets the true stars shine with ever-changing views of the ocean and mountains. Combined with a commitment to fresh, innovative cuisine, every meal here is transformed into an unforgettable occasion. The heavens seem much closer on Lord Howe.

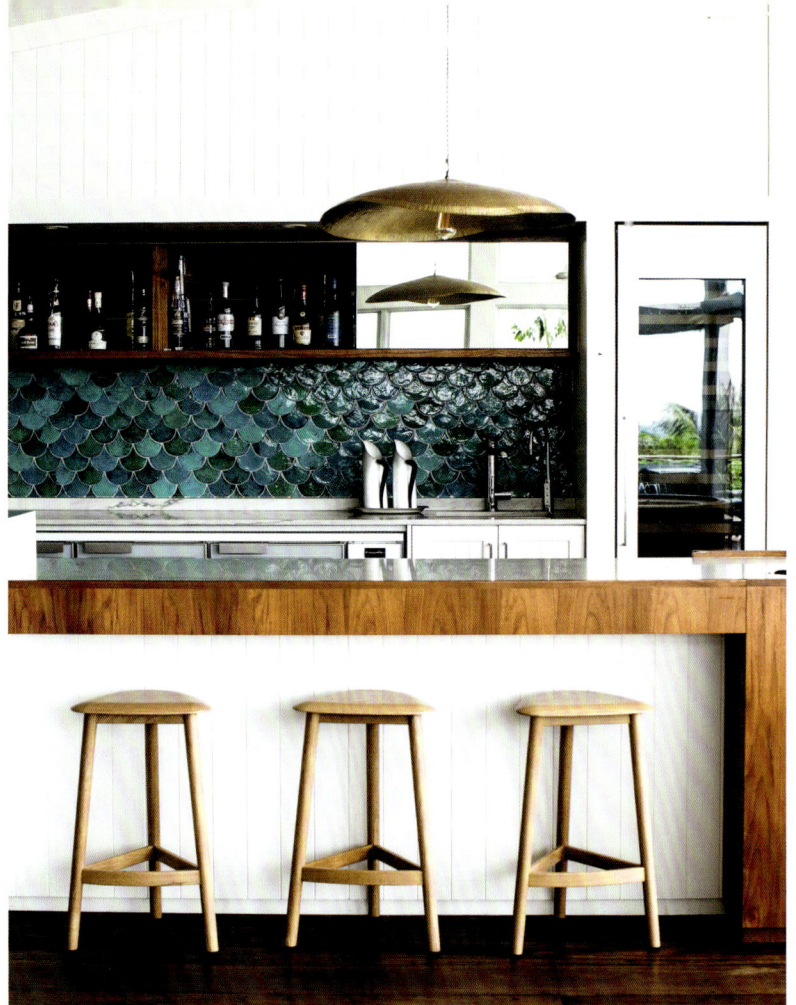

EXPLORE

• Get your hands dirty. Join the chef in the lodge's kitchen garden, visit the gardens of islanders who share their bounty on the lodge's menu, and forage for pea flowers and sea spinach at Blinky's Beach.

• Barbecuing is an art form on Lord Howe with wood-fired grills all over the island. Freshly caught fish, heritage farm greens and local craft beer, plus Capella's barbecue pack make it next level.

Kingfish with fennel, beetroot, ruby grapefruit, hot mustard and chickweed

SERVES 4-6 // PREP TIME 40 MINS (PLUS COOLING) // COOK 30 MINS

"On Lord Howe Island we are spoilt with an abundance of fresh fish especially line-caught kingfish," says executive chef Cooper Dickson. "The mustard in this dish works well with the raw fish and the ruby grapefruit offers a touch of citrus."

250	gm day-old sourdough bread
60	ml extra-virgin olive oil, plus extra for drizzling
1	baby fennel bulb (150gm)
2	tsp lemon juice
1	baby beetroot (50gm)
1	ruby grapefruit
½	tsp caster sugar
	Chickweed picked (see note)
300	gm sashimi-grade kingfish belly, thinly sliced

PICKLED BEETROOT

160	ml red wine vinegar
500	ml cold water
150	gm caster sugar
2	tbsp fine sea salt
1	bunch baby beetroot (500gm), scrubbed, trimmed, leaving 5cm stem

HOT MUSTARD YOGHURT

1	tsp hot English mustard
1½	tbsp lemon juice
140	gm Greek-style yoghurt
1	tbsp extra-virgin olive oil

1 For pickled beetroot, combine vinegar, water, sugar and salt in a small saucepan over medium heat; stir until sugar and salt dissolve. Add beetroot and cover with a cartouche to keep beetroot submerged. Bring to the boil then reduce heat to a simmer. Cook until beetroot are tender and can be easily pierced with a knife (25 minutes). Cool in pickling liquid, then peel and cut into sixths.

2 Meanwhile, for sourdough croûtons, preheat oven to 180°C. Remove crusts from bread. Tear bread into small pieces; place on an oven tray and drizzle with olive oil. Bake until golden (15 minutes). Cool.

3 For hot mustard yoghurt, combine ingredients in a bowl and season with salt. Refrigerate until required.

4 Using a mandolin, thinly shave fennel then place in a bowl with lemon juice and a pinch of salt; toss to coat. Thinly shave beetroot. Refrigerate fennel and beetroot separately until required.

5 Peel grapefruit with a sharp knife, then segment over a bowl to catch juices, and squeeze juice from remaining membrane; you will need 1 tbsp. Add sugar to grapefruit juice, whisk until dissolved, followed by olive oil, then season to taste.

6 Place croûtons, fennel, raw beetroot, grapefruit and chickweed in a bowl, drizzle with the dressing and toss gently to combine. Arrange salad, drained pickled beetroot and kingfish among plates then drizzle with hot mustard yoghurt.

NOTE Chickweed is an edible wild herbaceous weed that can be cooked like spinach or used as a salad green. If it's unavailable, substitute mâche (lamb's lettuce) or watercress.

PREPARE AHEAD Pickled beetroot and hot mustard yoghurt can be made a day ahead.

WINE MATCH 2014 Brown Brothers Patricia Pinot Noir Chardonnay Brut, King Valley, Vic.

Squid with sumac cream, olive salsa, peas and nasturtiums

SERVES 4 // PREP TIME 1 HR // COOK 5 MINS

"The smoky flavour of seafood cooked on a grill is hard to beat and at Capella we bring the spirit of Lord Howe's popular beachside barbecues to the table," says Dickson. "With salad ingredients harvested from the island's heritage farm, this dish sings of summer."

100   gm frozen edamame (see note)
100   gm podded peas (360gm unpodded)
100   gm crème fraîche
  1   tsp lemon zest
 ½   tsp sumac, plus extra for sprinkling
  4   whole arrow squid (150gm each),
      cleaned, tentacles reserved
      Extra-virgin olive oil, for drizzling
      Baby nasturtium leaves and flowers
      (see note), to serve

HERB OIL
  1   cup soft herbs (see note)
 80   ml extra-virgin olive oil

CHUNKY GREEN OLIVE SALSA
100   gm Sicilian green olives, pitted and
      coarsely chopped
      Finely grated zest of 1 lemon
  1   tbsp each chopped flat-leaf parsley,
      chives and dill
  1   small red shallot, finely chopped
  2   anchovy fillets, finely chopped
 60   ml extra-virgin olive oil

1 For herb oil, blanch herbs in a saucepan of boiling water for 15 seconds, drain and refresh in a bowl of iced water. Drain again and squeeze out excess water from herbs and pat dry with paper towel. Blend blanched herbs and olive oil in a high-speed blender until smooth. Strain through a fine sieve without applying any pressure. It will take 5 minutes for all the oil to drain through. Place herb oil into a screw-top jar and refrigerate until required.

2 For chunky green olive salsa, combine ingredients in a small bowl and season to taste. Refrigerate until required.

3 Blanch edamame and peas in a saucepan of boiling salted water until edamame are thawed and peas are bright green (2 minutes). Drain, refresh in a bowl of iced water, then drain again.

4 Stir crème fraîche, lemon zest and sumac together in a small bowl. Refrigerate until required.

5 Preheat a char-grill pan over medium-high heat. Drizzle squid and tentacles lightly with olive oil, season with salt, and cook until lightly charred and cooked through (1 minute each side).

6 To serve, thinly slice each squid, keeping pieces together. Place a squid and its tentacles on each plate, spoon sumac cream near squid and sprinkle with extra sumac. Place edamame, peas and olive salsa in a bowl and toss to combine. Spoon pea salad around squid, garnish with nasturtium leaves and flowers and drizzle with herb oil.

NOTE Frozen edamame are available from select Asian grocers and supermarkets. Nasturtiums are available from select greengrocers. For soft herbs, use remaining herbs from the bunches of flat-leaf parsley, chives and dill. You could also include tarragon, mint and chervil.

PREPARE AHEAD Herb oil and olive salsa can be made a day ahead.

WINE MATCH 2018 Yalumba The Virgilius Viognier, Eden Valley, SA.

Lizard Island

As the northernmost luxury island resort on the Great Barrier Reef, Lizard Island offers a unique resort-to-reef experience with an aquatic playground of activities, island dining and beachfront suites.

The arrival by private plane to exclusive Lizard Island is a good glimpse of the spectacular days ahead. As the plane lifts towards the watery horizon from Cairns in Queensland's tropical north, guests are treated to an aerial view of the Great Barrier Reef, with its many tiny islands, fringing reefs and remote cays. Seafaring adventures beckon and possibilities for exploring appear endless.

On approach, the plane rounds Lizard Island's pristine coasts where white-sand beaches fringe turquoise waters and the resort is revealed, set among tropical gardens.

Celebrated as the most northerly luxury island resort on the World Heritage-listed Great Barrier Reef, Lizard Island offers guests a walk-from-the-beach experience of the reef, with swimming, snorkelling or stand-up paddle-boarding an intimate way to encounter giant clams, turtles, magnificent coral and tropical fish just metres from the shore.

Motorised dinghies line the shallow waters by the beach club at Anchor Bay, ready to take guests on boating adventures to the island's many remote beaches. Towels, beach umbrellas, snorkel gear and gourmet hampers are packed to go, offering brunch or snacks and the essentials for a private beach safari: cool drinks and Champagne.

At the resort, 40 beach house-style suites are set among lush gardens with views of Anchor Bay or Sunset Beach. Inside the suites, fans turn languidly from high ceilings, while linen curtains frame floor-to-ceiling windows opening to verandahs with daybeds made for soaking in the view.

Cooled by the gentle sea breezes that whisper through tropical palms, the restaurant at Lizard Island is an open-air space to enjoy world-class island-inspired dining, its adjoining bar a natural hub for sunset drinks gatherings after a day's adventures.

The resort's all-inclusive, daily changing menu revolves around fresh, seasonal, local ingredients. The kitchen team works with Queensland's smaller producers who grow premium organic ingredients in the region's food bowl, which stretches from the Daintree Rainforest north to Cairns and west to the Atherton Tablelands. The menu features local seafood, beef, tropical mango and lime. Guests can sample coral trout, Spanish mackerel and line-caught tuna for a true taste of Queensland's tropical north or have their own catch prepared by the kitchen after their fishing trip. Sustainable fresh produce is key for the kitchen team who forage for natural island ingredients to add a unique native flavour to the tropics-inspired culinary offering.

EXPLORE

• Go fishing for coral trout, Spanish mackerel or tuna and ask the Lizard Island kitchen to prepare your catch for dinner.

• Dine in one of the lantern-lit private beach pavilions. Feel the sand between your toes and listen to the soft lapping of water just metres away.

Hibachi-grilled calamari, tomato kombu, green tomato pico de gallo

SERVES 4 // PREP TIME 30 MINS (PLUS COOLING) // COOK 1 HR 15 MINS

"Pico de gallo is how we utilise unripe tomatoes on the island, it is more like a salsa fresca, to which we add fish sauce for more of an umami flavour and brown sugar to balance. It is a mixture of a nahm jim dressing and tomato," says executive chef Winston Fong.

3   calamari (300gm each)

TOMATO KOMBU
500 ml fresh tomato juice
10   gm kombu (see note)
3   tsp balsamic vinegar
3   tsp Worcestershire sauce
1   tsp Tabasco

GREEN TOMATO PICO DE GALLO
3   green heirloom tomatoes (450gm), seeded
2   garlic cloves, finely chopped
3   tsp fish sauce
½   small golden shallot, finely diced
3   tsp lime juice
3   tsp brown sugar
1½ tbsp extra-virgin olive oil
    Fried curry leaves, crisp shallots and blanched charred spring onions

1 To make tomato kombu, place ingredients in a saucepan over medium heat, bring to the boil, then reduce heat to low and simmer gently until reduced by half (45 minutes). Refrigerate until required.

2 Meanwhile, to clean calamari, using a slight twisting motion, pull head firmly away from body; most entrails will come out as well. To remove head, cut the tentacles from the head, just below the eyes. Using your fingers, push out the hard black beak in centre of tentacles. Reserve tentacles for another use. Pull out and discard the clear quill that runs down the inside of the calamari body (hood). Rinse hoods well. Pull membrane away from the hood and flaps. Wash hood and flaps well. To help with gripping, dip your fingers in salt. Cut hoods down one side; open out and pat dry. Score the inside lightly with a small sharp knife in a criss-cross pattern without cutting all the way through, then cut into 2.5cm x 5cm pieces. Pat dry with paper towel. Refrigerate until required.

3 To make green tomato pico de gallo, blend ingredients to a coarse consistency.

4 Cook calamari on a hibachi grill over medium heat, continuously basting with tomato kombu mixture until calamari is caramelised (8 minutes).

5 Place green tomato pico de gallo on plates and top with calamari, fried curry leaves, crisp shallots and blanched chargrilled spring onions.

NOTE Kombu, dried seaweed, is available from Japanese grocers.

PREPARE AHEAD Pico de gallo and tomato kombu can be made a day head.

WINE MATCH 2020 Sirromet Granit Vermentino, Granite Belt, Qld.

Marinated scallops, curry oil, pickled rockmelon, finger lime and Thai basil

SERVES 4-6 // PREP TIME 25 MINS // COOK 10 MINS (PLUS INFUSING)

"When I worked in Fiji there were a lot of curry spices, so we combined tropical fruit with natural ingredients for a clean taste," says Fong. "We make this recipe with pink guava, which holds its own against aromatic curry oil. Rockmelon is a good substitute here."

18	scallops on the half shell, roe removed
2	finger limes, split, pearls removed
¼	cup small Thai basil leaves

CURRY OIL

100	ml grapeseed oil
1	small golden shallot (50gm), thinly sliced
1	garlic clove, thinly sliced
2	tsp finely chopped fresh turmeric
2	tsp cumin seeds
2	cloves
2	cardamom pods, bruised
1	cup curry leaves
3	tsp fish sauce
2	tsp brown sugar
1	tsp lime juice

PICKLED ROCKMELON

1	tbsp water
20	gm honey
1	tbsp white wine vinegar
¼	small rockmelon (400gm)

1 To make curry oil, heat 60ml of the grapeseed oil in a saucepan over low heat. Add shallot and garlic and cook, stirring occasionally, until onion is translucent (8 minutes). Add spices and curry leaves and stir until fragrant and cooked out (5 minutes). Remove pan from the heat, add the remaining oil and set aside to infuse (1 hour). Strain through a fine sieve into a bowl, discard solids and reserve curry oil.

2 To season curry oil, add fish sauce, brown sugar and lime juice to curry oil and whisk to combine.

3 To make pickled rockmelon, place water, honey and vinegar in a small saucepan and bring to the boil. Meanwhile, peel, seed and slice rockmelon and place in a heatproof bowl. Pour over pickling liquid and set aside in the fridge until required or for up to a day.

4 To serve, remove scallops from shells and clean shells. Slice each scallop into 3 pieces horizontally. Combine scallops and curry oil and marinate for 3 minutes. Place three scallop shells on each plate. Distribute scallop evenly among shells, discarding excess oil. Add pickled rockmelon and finger lime pearls, then garnish with Thai basil.

NOTE Double the curry oil and keep the leftovers refrigerated for up to 2 weeks to marinate any seafood you like.

PREPARE AHEAD Curry oil and pickled rockmelon can be made a day ahead.

WINE MATCH 2020 d'Arenberg The Dry Dam Riesling, multi-regional SA.

Qualia

True to its Latin name, Qualia resort spoils the senses with its understated luxury, enviable Whitsundays location and exclusive culinary and sensory experiences.

Qualia, a Latin word meaning "a collection of sensory experiences", is nestled in the northernmost tip of Hamilton Island in the Great Barrier Reef. Distinctly Australian in its understated style, this ultra-sophisticated escape with its enviable location and intuitive service, makes it an internationally renowned luxury destination. It's a truly special place where everything has been meticulously considered to relax the mind and spoil the senses.

Designed by Chris Beckingham to stimulate the senses and make the most of its tranquil natural surroundings, Qualia offers a harmonious sanctuary in the Whitsundays. Guests can choose to stay at one of the 60 chic pavilions, including the Windward Pavilions, each with ocean views and a private infinity plunge pool or the Leeward Pavilions with alfresco sundecks. For those seeking uncompromising luxury and privacy, the Beach House with spectacular views of the Coral Sea and its own guest pavilion, entertaining area and private swimming pool is the ultimate escape.

Qualia's pivotal design is the Long Pavilion, an epic space with floor-to-ceiling windows that open onto panoramic views, lined on one side by a pool. Built with Bowen granite, kwila hardwood floors and plantation hoop pine ceilings, the Long Pavilion houses the dining room, lounge, bar and library areas. Guests also enjoy access to a spa, gymnasium and two pools to complete the full range of high-end experiences offered at the resort.

The Long Pavilion's dining room provides relaxed, casual breakfasts and dinners while fine-dining restaurant, Pebble Beach, offers guests a tasting menu that highlights local seasonal produce.

To enrich the dining experience, Qualia offers private Talk and Taste sessions, food- and wine-led experiences hosted by its executive chef and sommelier. Each culinary journey, whether it's sake and sashimi, Champagne and freshly shucked oysters or wine and cheese, features the finest local and international produce curated to satisfy even the most discerning palate.

For a sensory experience that feels like it was designed for James Bond himself, the Journey to the Heart experience is exclusive to guests of Qualia and Hamilton Island. After a 30-minute scenic helicopter flight over Whitehaven Beach, Hill Inlet and the Great Barrier Reef, up to six guests arrive at the private Heart Island pontoon and board a custom-built, futuristic glass-bottomed boat, before making the short journey to explore Heart Reef and swim and snorkel in neighbouring lagoons.

EXPLORE

• Channel James Bond and take a helicopter flight over Whitehaven Beach to an exclusive pontoon just metres from iconic Heart Reef. With capacity for six guests, Heart Island also offers the opportunity to explore the Great Barrier Reef's coral from a glass-bottomed boat or by snorkelling.

• Hop on a complimentary electric golf buggy to Hamilton Island's One Tree Hill lookout to enjoy sunset drinks and Whitsundays' views.

Moreton Bay bug salad with yellow bean dressing

SERVES 4 // PREP TIME 45 MINS // COOK 15 MINS

"Designed around Qualia's ethos of sourcing Australia's best produce, this dish is filled with flavour and offers a balance of fresh, citrus notes paired with the slight sweetness of nahm jim dressing," says executive chef John Kennedy.

8 small raw Moreton Bay bugs (180gm each)
  Olive oil
  Lemon juice, to taste
1 green mango, peeled and cut into julienne
½ small green papaya, peeled and cut into julienne
50 gm red and yellow cherry tomatoes, halved
¼ cup each coriander, round mint and Vietnamese mint
½ pink grapefruit, segmented
1 red shallot, thinly sliced
2 tbsp lightly toasted coconut flakes

YELLOW BEAN DRESSING
1 garlic clove
1 long red chilli, seeded
1½ tbsp finely grated ginger
60 ml light soy sauce
90 gm honey
60 ml coconut vinegar (see note)
60 ml Shaoxing wine
2 tbsp yellow bean paste (see note)
2 tbsp finely grated palm sugar
½ tsp sesame oil

NAHM JIM
2 tsp finely grated ginger
1 tsp finely chopped garlic
1 tsp finely chopped long red chilli
2 tbsp sesame oil
80 ml peanut oil
2 tbsp soy sauce
1 tsp finely chopped pickled ginger
1 tsp pickled ginger juice
1½ tsp caster sugar
2 tbsp freshly squeezed lime juice
1 tbsp finely chopped Vietnamese mint

1 Separate the head from the tail of the bugs by twisting. Remove the tail meat from the shell by cutting the softer underside open with strong scissors. Gently pull the tail meat out, cut it in half lengthways and remove the digestive tract. Refrigerate until required.

2 Meanwhile, for yellow bean dressing, place ingredients in a blender and blend to a paste. Transfer mixture to a small saucepan and cook, stirring over low heat to infuse and dissolve sugar (5 minutes). Makes 300ml. Cool. Refrigerate until required.

3 Meanwhile, for nahm jim, place ingredients in a bowl and whisk together. Taste and adjust the balance of seasoning to your preference, using the sugar, lime juice and salt to achieve it. Makes 180ml.

4 Preheat oven to 200°C. Heat a little olive oil in a large ovenproof frying pan over high heat, and cook bugs, turning occasionally, until light golden (1-2 minutes). Transfer pan to the oven and cook until cooked through (3-4 minutes). Season with lemon juice.

5 Meanwhile, combine mango, papaya, tomatoes, coriander, round mint, Vietnamese mint, grapefruit, shallot and coconut in a bowl. Add 1½ tbsp nahm jim and toss gently to combine. Spoon 2 tbsp yellow bean dressing in the base of serving bowls, top with salad and four bug halves for each bowl.

NOTE Coconut vinegar and yellow bean paste (hugan jiang or taucheo) are available from Asian grocers. If yellow bean paste isn't available, substitute hoisin sauce. Leftover nahm jim will keep refrigerated for 1 week.

PREPARE AHEAD Yellow bean dressing and nahm jim can be made a day ahead.

WINE MATCH 2019 Penfolds Yattarna Chardonnay, multi-regional, SA and Tas.

Rye bread and brown butter ice-cream

SERVES 8 // PREP TIME 30 MINS (PLUS COOLING, FREEZING) // COOK 30 MINS

"Unexpected earthy flavours with a hint of sweetness makes this dessert well suited to give a glimpse into Qualia's culinary offering," says Kennedy. "The unique flavours paired with the textures in this dish provide an unparalleled sensory experience."

500	ml milk
300	ml pouring cream
1	vanilla bean, split and seeds scraped
10	egg yolks
220	gm caster sugar
250	gm unsalted butter, chopped
225	gm piece rye bread, crusts removed, sliced and toasted

HONEYCOMB

220	gm caster sugar
2	tbsp water
20	gm glucose syrup or golden syrup
2	tsp bicarbonate of soda

HAZELNUT BRITTLE

110	gm caster sugar
2	tbsp water
	Pinch of sea salt
100	gm roasted hazelnuts, peeled

1 For ice-cream base, combine milk, cream and vanilla bean and seeds in a saucepan over medium heat and bring almost to the boil; remove from heat. Meanwhile, whisk egg yolks and sugar in a heatproof bowl until pale. Gradually ladle three to four ladlefuls of hot milk mixture over the egg yolks while whisking, then slowly pour in the rest of the milk mixture, while whisking. Return to pan and cook, stirring continuously, until mixture thickly coats a spoon (6-7 minutes) and reaches 80°C.

2 For beurre noisette, melt butter in a saucepan over medium heat until foamy and nut brown (4-6 minutes).

3 Strain ice-cream base into a storage tub. Add beurre noisette and toasted rye bread; cover and refrigerate overnight for flavours to develop.

4 Strain ice-cream mixture into a bowl; return one-sixth of the toasted rye bread to the ice-cream mixture and whisk to evenly combine. Churn in an ice-cream machine then transfer to a container and freeze until ready to serve.

5 For honeycomb, grease a 20cm square cake tin. Place sugar, water and glucose syrup in a heavy-based saucepan over low heat, stir without boiling until sugar dissolves. Increase heat to medium and simmer until a light caramel forms (6 minutes). Remove pan from heat, immediately add bicarb and stir in quickly to combine; the mixture will bubble vigorously. Pour into prepared tin and leave to cool. Store in an airtight container until required or for up to 1 week.

6 For hazelnut brittle, place sugar, water and salt in a small heavy-based saucepan over low heat, stir without boiling until sugar dissolves. Increase heat to medium and simmer until a light caramel forms. Remove pan from heat; stir in nuts, then pour onto a tray lined with baking paper; leave to cool. Store in an airtight container until required or for up to 1 week.

7 To serve, chop hazelnut brittle into coarse pieces with a sturdy knife and place on serving plates. Using two spoons dipped in boiling water, shape rye bread ice-cream into quenelles and divide among plates. Top ice-cream with crushed honeycomb.

PREPARE AHEAD Rye bread and brown butter ice-cream, honeycomb and hazelnut brittle can be made a day ahead.

WINE MATCH 2020 Voyager Estate Sparkling Chenin Blanc, Margaret River, WA.

Makepeace Island

Whether it's a relaxing escape or a fun-filled adventure,
Makepeace Island set in the tranquil waters of the Sunshine Coast offers
a heart-warming experience with exceptional dining.

There's a lot to love about heart-shaped Makepeace Island set in the tranquil waters of Noosa River on the Sunshine Coast. Combining modern contemporary living with traditional tropical island design, Makepeace creates a serene environment that is in complete harmony with nature. Whether you're looking for a multigenerational family getaway, corporate conference destination or wellness retreat, Makepeace offers a peaceful place to relax and unwind.

The island's natural heart-shaped coastline sets the tone for your island experience with the island's hashtag #lovemakepeace filtering its way into your every experience. With its luxury Balinese-style accommodation, stunning natural landscape, proximity to Noosa Heads and five-star service and food, it is easy to see why guests love Makepeace Island.

Makepeace's kitchen team creates bespoke menus from local produce as it works closely with regional producers to ensure that its seasonally driven menus use only the best the Sunshine Coast has to offer. The result? Culinary adventures in collaboration with guests that become a high point of their stay. Guests can dine on sashimi tuna with pickled cape gooseberry, shiso and white miso or grilled octopus with potato, white anchovy, celery, tomato, lemon and saffron or a salad of bamboo shoots, water chestnut, wakame, cucamelons and myoga. For those interested in a little hands-on cooking, guests (both young and old) have the opportunity to take a masterclass with either the island's executive chef or pastry chef.

A mere 10-minute boat ride to Noosa Marina or 15-minute trip to Noosa's bustling Hastings Street, Makepeace is ideally situated on the doorstep of the Sunshine Coast. Sleeping up to 22 guests, exclusive use of Makepeace Island includes three oversized two-bedroom luxury villas, four spacious ensuite rooms in the Island House and the Boathouse with its waterfront views of the north shore. Each room and villa has its own private deck with views. A special butler bath service is also available to villa guests for their oversized carved volcanic rock baths.

The beauty of Makepeace Island lies in the opportunity to explore as much or as little as you like. While some guests may choose to simply relax and recharge, others can take advantage of both on- and off-island experiences such as stand-up paddle boarding, kayaking, river fishing, swimming in its 500,000-litre freshwater pool, walking trails, sunset cruises, beach picnics, gym and tennis court. With exclusive access to your own island, standout culinary offerings and plenty of things to do, what's not to love?

EXPLORE

• Hands-on masterclasses with the chef, tailored to suit your tastes and kitchen skills, are available for both adults and children.

• Explore the Noosa Everglades, one of only two everglade environments in the world. Paddle by kayak through spectacular scenery for some impressive birdwatching.

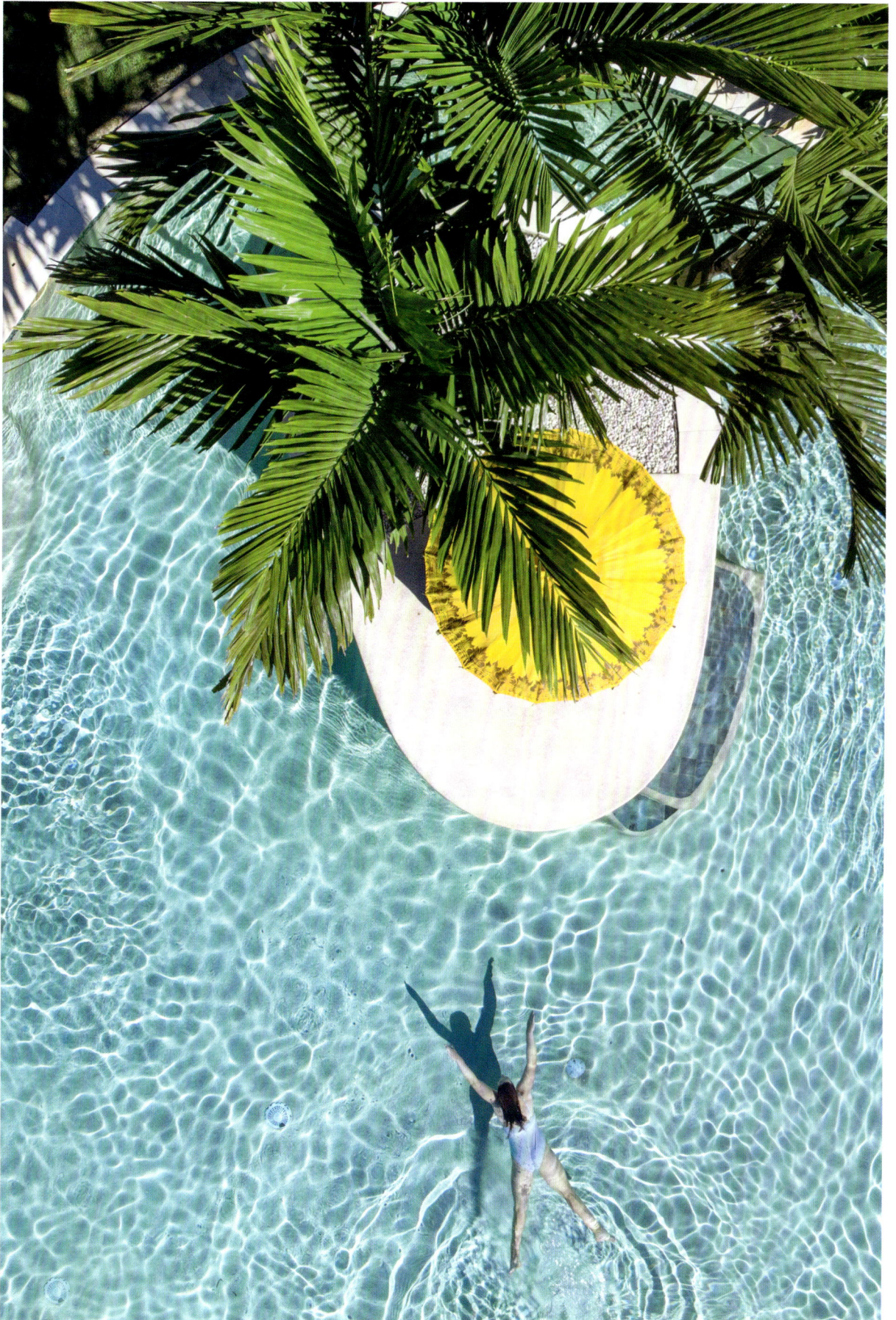

Crayfish with coral butter, potato and crisp artichoke salad, radishes with rosella dressing and shio koji cream

SERVES 2 // PREP TIME 1 HR // COOK 45 MINS

"Painted crayfish is a luxury – we respect produce and use as much of it as possible," says executive chef Zeb Gilbert. "The body, shell and coral, all of it is integral to the dish. Guests gather around the fire to watch us grill the local sustainable seafood."

CRAYFISH, MANDARIN AND CORAL BUTTER

- 2 kg painted crayfish, chilled in the freezer for 30 minutes and spiked (see note)
- 100 gm unsalted butter, at room temperature
- Zest of ¼ mandarin
- Lime half and salt flakes

POTATO AND CRISP ARTICHOKE SALAD

- 300 gm heritage potatoes (see note), peeled and sliced into rounds
- 3 garlic cloves, peeled and crushed
- 1 sprig each thyme and oregano
- 350 ml extra-virgin olive oil
- 1 lemon, zested into thin strips
- 2 tsp lemon juice
- 1 tbsp capers
- 150 gm Jerusalem artichokes
- 200 ml rice bran oil
- 20 each oregano and Lebanese cress leaves (see note)

RADISHES WITH ROSELLA DRESSING AND SHIO KOJI CREAM

- 4 radishes
- 60 ml mirin
- 50 ml rosella vinegar (see note) or red wine vinegar
- 60 ml extra-virgin olive oil
- 1½ tsp Dijon mustard
- 2 tbsp shio koji (see note)
- 180 gm sour cream

1 To clean crayfish, flip crayfish over with the head facing away from you. Gently insert kitchen scissors between the tail and the head. Cut upwards, splitting the head then cut the join between the head and the tail. Wiggle the tail gently to remove from the head. Reserve the head. On the belly side of the crayfish, cut up each side and peel the belly shell back. Remove meat from tail, reserve tail shell, rinse in salty water and reserve for serving. Remove the intestinal tract and run a metal skewer along either side of the tail so it remains flat during cooking. Refrigerate until required.

2 For coral butter, split the crayfish head in half and remove the 2 bright orange coral lobes with a teaspoon. Pass the coral through a fine sieve into a small bowl. Add butter, mandarin zest, salt and pepper, and combine. Leave soft and spreadable at room temperature.

3 For potato and crisp artichoke salad, place potatoes, garlic, thyme, oregano and a pinch of salt and pepper in a saucepan and cover with olive oil. Poach until potatoes are tender (20 minutes). Combine lemon zest and juice and capers in a bowl and season to taste. Remove potatoes from oil with a slotted spoon and combine with the dressing in the bowl.

4 For crisp artichokes, scrub and slice artichokes thinly on a mandolin, rinse in water and pat dry on paper towel. Heat rice bran oil in a saucepan to 170°C. Fry artichokes, in small batches, until golden and crisp (3-5 minutes), remove with a slotted spoon and drain on paper towel. Season to taste.

5 For radishes with rosella dressing, trim radishes leaving a few small leaves intact, then thinly slice on a mandolin. Refrigerate under damp paper towel until required. Bring mirin to the boil in a small saucepan to burn off the alcohol. Whisk 1 tbsp of the mirin with vinegar, olive oil and mustard together in a small bowl. Season if needed.

6 For shio koji cream, whisk remaining 2 tbsp mirin with shio koji and sour cream until combined. Check seasoning and adjust if needed. Refrigerate until required.

7 Preheat a charcoal grill to medium heat; grill crayfish tail, brushing liberally and often with the coral butter or until slightly undercooked (15 minutes). Remove and set aside for a few minutes to finish cooking. Cut tail meat into medallions; return to the reserved shell and brush with a little more butter. Place on a plate with lime half and salt flakes.

8 To serve potato salad, arrange dressed potatoes in a bowl with oregano and Lebanese cress. Garnish with crisp artichokes.

9 To serve radishes, spread shio koji cream in the base of a bowl. Dip radishes in rosella dressing and arrange on top.

10 Serve crayfish with potato and radish salads to share.

NOTE Painted crayfish is also known as tropical rock lobster. If it's unavailable, substitute other species of rock lobster. For heritage potatoes, choose blue congo, midnight moon and pink fir apple potatoes. Lebanese cress, which tastes like carrots, is available from select greengrocers. If it's unavailable, substitute flat-leaf parsley or green carrot tops. The rosella plant's edible red calyxes (fruit) have a tart sweet taste and are often preserved in syrup. Shio koji is an all-purpose seasoning with an umami flavour made by inoculating grains such as rice, barley or soy beans with koji kin, a form of mould.

WINE MATCH 2016 Tyrrell's Vat 1 Semillon, Hunter Valley, NSW.

Chocolate sorbet, kinako gelée, cacao nib

SERVES 8 // PREP TIME 2 HRS (PLUS SETTING, CHURNING) // COOK 3 HRS

Cacao nibs and freeze-dried sour
cherries, to serve

CHOCOLATE SORBET
600 ml water
220 gm caster sugar
50 gm Dutch-process cocoa
50 gm dark chocolate (70% cocoa solids)
Pinch of sea salt flakes

CHOCOLATE MERINGUE
2 eggwhites
110 gm caster sugar
10 gm Dutch-process cocoa

KINAKO GELÉE
30 ml espresso coffee
250 ml milk
35 gm kinako (see note)
2.5 titanium-strength gelatine leaves

TUILE
80 gm eggwhites
100 gm caster sugar
60 gm unsalted butter, melted
85 gm plain flour

CHOCOLATE CRUMB
100 gm unsalted butter
20 gm caster sugar
100 gm plain flour
10 gm Dutch-process cocoa

CHOCOLATE SNAP
85 gm caster sugar
30 gm liquid glucose
45 gm unsalted butter
20 gm plain flour
20 gm Dutch-process cocoa

SAKE CHERRIES
100 ml sake
25 gm caster sugar
100 gm dried sour cherries

1 For chocolate sorbet, bring water to the boil in a saucepan. Add sugar and sifted cocoa, bring to a gentle simmer and cook, whisking occasionally until dissolved (5 minutes). Remove from heat; stir in chocolate and salt until combined. Transfer to an airtight container and refrigerate until chilled (2 hours). Churn sorbet in an ice-cream maker. Transfer to an airtight container and freeze.

2 For chocolate meringue, preheat oven to 100°C. Whisk eggwhites using an electric mixer until soft peaks form, then gradually add sugar and beat until stiff peaks form and sugar dissolves. Sift in cocoa and whisk just until evenly combined. Line an oven tray with baking paper; spread meringue over tray in a 3mm-thick even layer. Bake until crisp (1½ hours). Cool then break into shards and store in an airtight container.

3 For kinako gelée, heat espresso, milk and kinako in a small saucepan until almost boiling. Soak gelatine leaves in a bowl of cold water until softened (3 minutes). Squeeze out excess water, add to the pan and stir until gelatine dissolves. Strain into a 15cm x 20cm container so mixture is 1cm deep. Refrigerate to set (4 hours). Cut gelée into 1cm square cubes then store in an airtight container in the fridge until required.

4 For tuile, preheat oven to 160°C. Place two narrow cylinders (bottle or rolling pin) in front of each other on a bench. Using a hand-held whisk, combine eggwhites and sugar in a bowl. Whisk in melted butter, then stir in flour until smooth. On a silicone baking mat (or baking paper-lined oven tray), using an overset spatula, spread batter in 6cm-wide strips as thinly as possible. Cook until just turning golden (6 minutes). Working quickly, drape tuiles over cylinders to create a wavy shape, then manipulate the tuiles into abstract shapes. (They will cool and harden very quickly.) Cool, then transfer to an airtight container until required.

5 For chocolate crumb, preheat oven to 180°C. Cream butter and sugar, sift in flour and cocoa, and combine well. Spread biscuit dough in a thin layer on a tray lined with baking paper and bake until set (25 minutes). Remove tray from oven. Using a fork, drag it through the hot biscuit to break it up into a chocolate crumb. Cool, then transfer to an airtight container until required.

6 For chocolate snap, preheat oven to 175°C. Stir sugar, glucose and butter in a saucepan over low-medium heat until melted and combined. Remove from heat, sift over flour and cocoa, and stir until combined. Place a 40cm sheet of baking paper on a bench, top with ¼ cup chocolate mix. Lay another sheet of baking paper on top and using a rolling pin, roll out until mixture is extremely thin and almost translucent. Remove top sheet of paper. Place the sheet with the chocolate mix onto an oven tray and bake until bubbles appear (5-7 minutes). Transfer chocolate snap on paper sheet to bench. Leave until cool and brittle. Once set, break into shards and stack in an airtight container separated by sheets of baking paper. Store in the freezer until required then use straight from the freezer.

7 For sake cherries, stir sake and sugar in a small saucepan until sugar dissolves and mixture boils. Pour over dried cherries in a heatproof container. Leave to steep for at least 1 hour or until required.

8 To serve, place 1 tbsp chocolate crumb in the base of each serving bowl. Top each with a few shards of chocolate meringue, 5 cubes of kinako gelée, 7 sake cherries and sprinkle with cacao nibs. Place a quenelle of chocolate sorbet in bowls then layer chocolate snap and tuile on top, adding height to the dish. Using a Microplane, grate freeze-dried cherries over each dessert.

NOTE Kinako, roasted soybean powder, is available from Asian grocers.

PREPARE AHEAD All dessert components can be made up to 2 days ahead.

WINE MATCH NV Montalto Pennon Hill Sparkling Rosé, Mornington Peninsula, Vic.

Saffire Freycinet

Perched along the sandy coastline linking the Freycinet Peninsula with Tasmania, Saffire offers a luxury retreat with unique immersive experiences and a fine-dining offering that celebrates local produce.

For eleven years, Saffire Freycinet has been a shining beacon in the Australian luxury travel scene. Since its inception, its purpose has been to create memorable guest experiences as well as showcase the very best that the Freycinet Peninsula and Tasmania have to offer.

Saffire is located on the inside of the gentle curve of sandy coastline that joins the Freycinet Peninsula to mainland Tasmania. Saffire overlooks the wide expanses of Great Oyster Bay, where migrating whales and dolphins come to play; calamari and squid in-season spawn in the rocky outcrops; local farms produce fresh, succulent oysters in some of the world's cleanest waters; and fishing boats and trawlers bring in their daily catch of rock lobster, scallops and deep-sea fish.

Saffire's 20 suites are discreetly positioned overlooking the Hazards Mountains, Freycinet Peninsula and the pristine waters of Great Oyster Bay. The dominant view from Saffire's every window is the pink-hued granite of the Hazards Mountains, providing a spectacular and ever-changing backdrop from morning to nightfall. Guests can also enjoy Saffire's exclusive day spa, restaurant and lounge.

Saffire's Palate Restaurant focuses on the very best local produce with oysters and mussels from Great Oyster Bay and a daily supply of local crayfish, scallops and deep-sea fish. The daily changing tasting menu, paired with outstanding local cool-climate wines, is created from produce available fresh from the sea or paddock that day.

Distinct in its design and exclusive in its features, Saffire sets itself apart as the best luxury accommodation in Tasmania with its approach to tailored one-on-one experiences and service.

Guests can choose from a range of unique experiences that seek to connect them to place through nature, produce and culture. For the Saffire Beekeeping Experience, don an apiarist suit to extract fresh honeycomb from nearby hives under the guidance of Saffire horticulturalist, Rob Barker. Stand knee-deep in waders for the Freycinet Marine Farm Experience to shuck oysters straight from the water while guides explain the internationally significant wetland and the life cycle of oysters. For the Tasmanian Devil Experience, visit Saffire's open-range Tasmanian devil enclosure to experience a rare encounter with the world's largest carnivorous marsupials. Take a coastal walk with Indigenous guide, Mick Quilliam, to sample local bush tucker and discover the history of the Oyster Bay people in the Connection to Country Experience. These experiences play a key role in connecting guests to the Freycinet Peninsula.

EXPLORE

• Sample prized Pacific oysters shucked straight from their beds. Slip on a pair of waders and head out into the wetlands and waters of a nearby working oyster farm to enjoy spectacular views, oysters and sparkling Tassie wine.

• The Wineglass Bay walk is a Freycinet highlight but to enjoy the hike with an indulgent gourmet picnic and chauffeured return trip aboard the Saffire vessel is a must-do.

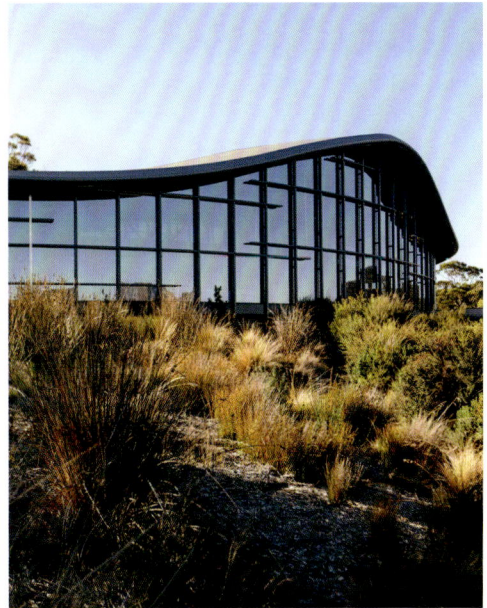

Buckwheat soba, lobster tail, roasted cashew and pickled cucumber

SERVES 4-6 // PREP TIME 1 HR (PLUS STANDING) // COOK 1 HR

200 gm raw cashews
4 raw Bay lobsters or Moreton Bay bugs (250gm each; see note)
1 tbsp Wadaman Gold sesame oil (see note)
2 nori sheets
1 bunch coriander

BUCKWHEAT SOBA
250 gm buckwheat flour
100 gm "00" flour
175 ml mineral water
 Tapioca starch, for rolling the noodles

PICKLED CUCUMBER
100 ml yuzu juice
1 tbsp rice wine vinegar
1 tbsp white sugar
2 Lebanese cucumbers

SESAME DRESSING
140 gm white sesame seeds
25 ml yuzu juice
25 ml white tamari
25 ml Wadaman Gold sesame oil
2 tsp rice wine vinegar
2 tsp mirin

1 For buckwheat soba, combine buckwheat and "00" flours in a large bowl. Add mineral water, and, using your hands, knead together until mixture forms a crumbly dough. Turn out onto a bench, continue kneading until a firm, dry dough forms (5 minutes). You may need to add an extra teaspoon of water if the dough seems too dry. Loosely wrap dough in plastic wrap and set aside on the bench to rest for at least 30 minutes.

2 Meanwhile, preheat oven to 140°C. Roast cashews until golden (40 minutes). Cool, then using the base of a saucepan, lightly crush cashews.

3 To prepare Bay lobsters, using a clean cloth in each hand, pull the tails off the bugs. You can freeze the shells for a stock for another time. Using a pair of sturdy scissors, cut down the inside of the tail shell on each side and remove that section. Gently ease out the tail meat then remove the intestinal tract. Refrigerate until required.

4 For pickled cucumber, stir yuzu, vinegar and sugar in a small saucepan over medium heat until sugar dissolves and mixture boils. Cool. Meanwhile, peel cucumbers and halve lengthways. Using a small spoon, scoop out seeds and discard, then slice cucumber and place in a bowl. Pour pickling liquid over cucumber and refrigerate to pickle (1 hour or until required).

5 To make noodles, dust a bench and rolling pin with tapioca starch. Using the palm of your hand flatten buckwheat dough. Using a rolling pin or pasta machine, roll out the dough as thinly as possible (3mm), repeating dusting the bench and rolling pin to prevent the dough sticking. Roll the dough up like a swiss roll. Using a sharp, thin-bladed knife, slice the roll as thinly as possible into 2mm-thick noodles. Dust noodles with tapioca to prevent them from sticking to each other.

6 To cook noodles, bring a large saucepan of salted water to the boil and cook noodles in two batches until they float to the top (2 minutes). Drain noodles, then refresh under cold running water. Allow excess water to drain off then place in a large bowl, drizzle with sesame oil and toss to combine.

7 For sesame dressing, place sesame seeds in a frying pan, place pan over medium heat, and cook, stirring until golden (5 minutes). Transfer to a mortar and pestle and pound to a rough paste. Stir in yuzu juice, tamari, sesame oil, rice wine vinegar and mirin then season to taste if you need with a little salt. Makes 200ml.

8 Roughly tear nori sheets into pieces, place in a high-speed blender and blend on medium speed to a coarse powder. Pick the nicest coriander leaves off the bunch and reserve to serve.

9 To cook Bay lobsters aburi style, place an oiled wire rack over an oven tray and place Bay lobsters on top. Using a blow torch, burn all sides of the lobster tails (30 seconds). Cut Bay lobsters in half lengthways then using the blow torch, burn the cut surface too (1 minute). Slice each tail half into 4 pieces.

10 Gently tease out the noodles in case they have stuck together and dress well with the sesame dressing. Add drained pickled cucumber and cashews. Using clean hands, toss mixture together and place a bundle of the noodle, cucumber and cashew mix in each bowl, then top each with a sliced bug tail. Sprinkle with nori powder and garnish with coriander leaves.

NOTE To cook the lobsters in this manner they must be impeccably fresh, if in doubt make sure to cook them all the way through. Wadaman Gold sesame oil, made in Osaka using a laborious process that results in a delicate and nuanced oil, is available from providerstore.com.au. If it's unavailable, substitute other sesame oils.

PREPARE AHEAD Sesame dressing can be made a day ahead.

WINE MATCH 2014 Josef Chromy Zdar Chardonnay, Tamar Valley, Tas.

Freycinet Marine Farm black mussels, tomato broth, shellfish mayonnaise and crisp herbs

SERVES 8 // PREP TIME 1 HR (PLUS STANDING, COOLING) // COOK 1 HR 45 MINS

"Saffire looks out over Great Oyster Bay, which is the same body of water in which Freycinet Marine Farm harvests their incredible black mussels," says executive chef Iain Todd. "In this recipe we feature these mussels in their purest form straight from the bay."

2 kg Freycinet Marine Farm black mussels, scrubbed, beards removed
60 ml water
¼ cup dill sprigs
¼ cup flat-leaf parsley leaves
¼ cup French tarragon
Olive oil cooking spray

TOMATO BROTH
500 gm ripe red tomatoes
2 red capsicums
2 red onions
4 garlic cloves
2 tbsp Ashbolt extra-virgin olive oil, plus extra to serve
3 thyme sprigs

SHELLFISH MAYONNAISE
500 ml grapeseed oil
1 garlic clove
1 thyme sprig
1 bay leaf
3 egg yolks
3 tsp rice wine vinegar
1 tsp smoked paprika

1 Place mussels and water in a large, deep frying pan (in 2 batches if necessary), cover with a lid; cook, shaking the pan occasionally until mussels open (2-3 minutes). Strain mussels and reserve the cooking liquid (600ml). Spread mussels out over an oven tray then place in the freezer for 5 minutes to arrest the cooking.

2 Once cool, remove the meat from the shells and discard any pea crabs and remaining bits of beard. Reserve the mussel shells.

3 For tomato broth, preheat oven to 220°C. Roughly chop tomatoes, capsicum, onions, and garlic. Place on an oven tray, drizzle with olive oil and scatter with thyme sprigs then season to taste. Bake until the vegetables are burnished golden brown (25-30 minutes). Discard herbs.

4 Blend vegetables and cooking juices with reserved mussel cooking liquid in a high-speed blender until a brothy soupy consistency. Strain mixture through a fine sieve, then strain again through a coffee filter or sieve lined with muslin. Discard solids. Refrigerate broth until required. Makes 500ml.

5 Place half the mussel shells in a single layer on an oven tray and bake at 220°C until pale, shiny and brittle (30 minutes). Remove from oven. Using the end of a rolling pin or hammer, smash the shells into small pieces.

6 For shellfish mayonnaise, place mussel shell pieces, grapeseed oil, garlic, thyme and bay in a small saucepan. Cook over the lowest heat possible to infuse the flavours of the roasted shells into the oil without it getting so hot that the heat destroys the delicate flavour notes (30 minutes). Remove from the heat and cool. Once cool, strain through a fine sieve lined with cheesecloth over a jug (discard solids).

7 To finish shellfish mayonnaise, place egg yolks, vinegar and smoked paprika in the jug of a stick blender, then blend well. Gradually add the mussel shell oil, drop by drop, at first until starting to thicken, then in a slow steady stream until thick and emulsified. Season well with salt. Spoon into a container and refrigerate until required.

8 Working in batches, place dill sprigs, parsley leaves and tarragon, in a single layer on a large plate lined with paper towel and spray lightly with oil. Microwave on medium (80% power) for 1½ minutes or until dried. Repeat with remaining herbs and paper towel. Transfer to an airtight container until required.

9 To serve, gently warm the tomato broth in a saucepan. Divide soup among wide shallow bowls, arrange the mussels over the base and top each with a little shellfish mayonnaise and a dried herb. Spoon a few drops of olive oil around the broth.

PREPARE AHEAD Tomato broth and shellfish mayonnaise can be made a day ahead.

WINE MATCH 2019 Mandoon Estate Sparkling, Swan Valley, WA.

True North

A luxury vessel sailing the Kimberley and beyond promises a trip of a lifetime with its endless possibilities for exploration, destination-inspired dining, adventure boats and onboard helicopter.

An adventure on the luxury vessel *True North* is not a typical expedition cruise. For more than 30 years, the *True North* has been navigating unique sailing experiences, taking guests on adventure-cruises around the magnificent Australian coastline and stunning waters of Indonesia and Papua New Guinea. Custom-built and designed to sail off the beaten track, *True North* takes guests on adventures designed to uncover hidden coastal gems in luxurious comfort.

Sailing on the *True North* is like travelling in a five-star hotel on the water with its three decks of 18 cabins each with satellite telephones. Accommodation includes four stateroom cabins and six double cabins with king-size beds, large windows and ensuites and eight twin cabins on the lower deck with portholes and ensuites. The service onboard this adventure yacht is impeccable with an Australian crew of 22 taking care of just 36 guests.

With six dedicated adventure boats and an onboard seven-seater Eurocopter, guests can choose whether to spend the day catching barramundi with a wide selection of complimentary fishing equipment or perhaps fly to an otherwise impossible-to-reach spot. Whether witnessing the majesty of the Kimberley coast, experiencing the hospitality of the South Pacific or sightseeing around Sydney, the *True*

North will take you there in nautical style and comfort. Other destinations include the still-wild coast of Western Australia, the islands of Raja Ampat, mysterious Bougainville and the Eyre Peninsula.

Extended periods at sea are specifically excluded and activity-based itineraries provide the ultimate opportunity for guests to experience the destination. Every day on the *True North* is an activity day and activities can include walks, fishing, snorkelling, diving, picnics, natural history and cultural events.

At 50 metres in length, the *True North* is purpose-built to navigate wilderness areas that are not accessible to bigger ships. Adventure boats take guests away in small groups to experience wilderness up-close and the luxury of numerous tenders also means that guests have greater opportunity to explore whenever they wish.

The dining experience on the *True North* is sustainable and destination-inspired. The *True North*'s fish congee is an onboard favourite based on the original recipe introduced by one of its founding chefs more than 30 years ago. It features the fish of the day (mangrove jack, barramundi or fingermark bream) with lemongrass, chilli, sesame oil, coriander and ginger. Another signature dish is *True North*'s seafood laksa, a popular light lunch.

EXPLORE

• Go beyond the galley and accompany the chefs as they land the catch of the day for a true sea-to-plate dining experience.

• From the Rowley Shoals to Ningaloo Reef and the Abrolhos Islands, take off on one of *True North*'s adventure boats for an unforgettable snorkel or dive.

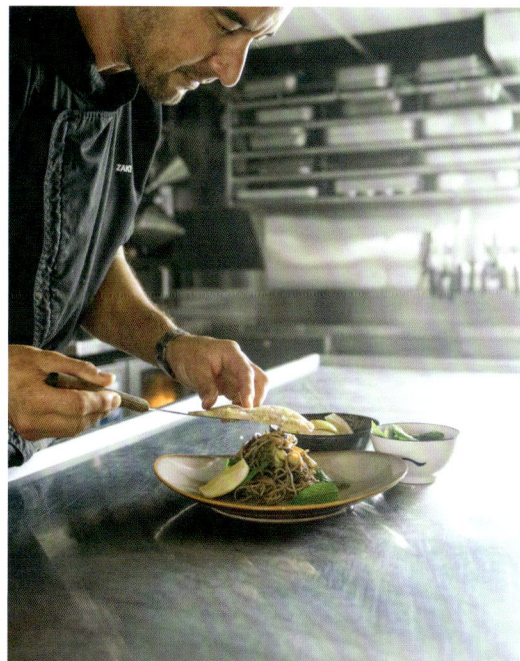

Fish congee

SERVES 6 // PREP TIME 30 MINS // COOK 1 HR 50 MINS

"Congee is a signature dish on *True North* and has featured onboard for more than 30 years," says head chef Luke Pursell. "It has always been popular with guests as it showcases the impeccably fresh fish we source from the pristine waters around us."

1	bunch coriander
100	gm ginger
1	large onion
6	garlic cloves
1	lemongrass stalk, white part only
2	tbsp vegetable oil
2.5	litres fish stock
150	gm jasmine rice
60	ml fish sauce
800	gm skinless white-fleshed fish, cut into 2cm cubes
3	spring onions, sliced
1	long red chilli, thinly sliced
	Fried shallots, chilli sambal, pickled ginger, crushed peanuts, soy sauce and sesame oil, to serve

1 Pick leaves from coriander and transfer leaves to an airtight container, then refrigerate until required to serve. Roughly chop remaining stems and cleaned roots, then chop ginger, onion, garlic and lemongrass. Place in a food processor and blend to a fine paste.

2 Heat vegetable oil in a large saucepan over low-medium heat. Add paste and cook, stirring often, to cook out the flavours (5 minutes).

3 Add fish stock and rice to the pan and bring to the boil over high heat. Reduce heat to low-medium and simmer until the rice has broken down, stirring regularly, to avoid the rice catching on the base of the pan, and the congee has thickened and resembles a thin porridge (1¼-1½ hours).

4 Add fish sauce and fish to the congee and simmer until fish is just cooked through (5 minutes).

5 To serve, divide congee among bowls and top with spring onion, chilli, pickled ginger and fried shallots. Serve with bowls of reserved coriander leaves, crushed peanuts, chilli sambal, soy sauce and sesame oil to the side.

WINE MATCH 2019 De Bortoli The Estate Pinot Blanc, Yarra Valley, Vic.

Seafood laksa

SERVES 6 // PREP TIME 1 HR 30 MINS // COOK 1 HR 30 MINS

"While the recipe here features an abundance of our local seafood, it is possible to adapt the laksa base and replace the seafood with chicken," says Pursell. "For a vegetarian option, use vegetable stock, coconut amino for the fish sauce, and tofu."

75 gm fresh turmeric
100 gm ginger
2 lemongrass stalks, white part only
6 garlic cloves
6 makrut lime leaves
2 long green chillies
5 red shallots
1 bunch coriander, leaves picked, roots reserved
2 tbsp vegetable oil
2 litres chicken stock
1 litre coconut cream
90 gm finely grated palm sugar
60 ml fish sauce
50 ml lime juice
100 gm dried rice vermicelli
12 raw tiger prawns (500gm)
500 gm scallops
1 bunch bok choy
500 gm clams, purged of sand
800 gm firm-fleshed white fish, cut into 2cm cubes
2 tsp vegetable oil
125 gm bean sprouts
1 long red chilli, thinly sliced
50 gm fried shallot
90 gm roasted unsalted peanuts, crushed
1 lime, cut into wedges

1 Roughly chop turmeric, ginger, lemongrass, garlic, lime leaves, green chilli, shallots and coriander root. Place in a food processor and blend to a fine paste.
2 Heat vegetable oil in a large saucepan over low-medium heat. Add spice paste and cook, stirring often, to cook out the flavours (5 minutes). Add chicken stock and simmer gently (45 minutes). Makes 550ml.
3 Add coconut cream, palm sugar, fish sauce and lime juice, simmer gently without boiling for flavours to develop (20 minutes). If necessary, strain laksa sauce into another clean saucepan to remove any stringy pieces of lemongrass and ginger. Set aside.
4 Boil 1 litre of water and pour over rice noodles in a heatproof bowl and stand until noodles have softened (3-4 minutes), then drain and refresh under cold water.
5 Meanwhile, clean prawns leaving tails intact. Remove the muscle from the side of each scallop. Wash and shred bok choy. Strain off any remaining water from cooked rice noodles.
6 Divide bok choy and noodles among bowls. Bring laksa sauce back to the boil, add prawns, clams and fish and reduce heat to low. Cook, covered until seafood is just cooked through and clams open.
7 Meanwhile, heat oil in a large frying pan over medium-high heat and cook scallops for 30 seconds each side or until just cooked through. Divide among bowls.
8 Ladle laksa sauce and divide seafood evenly among bowls. Garnish soup with bean sprouts, red chilli, fried shallot and crushed peanuts and serve with lime wedges and picked coriander leaves to the side.

PREPARE AHEAD Recipe can be made up until the end of step 3 a day ahead.

WINE MATCH 2020 St Hugo Eden Valley Riesling, Eden Valley, SA.

AMONG THE TREES

Unwind and reconnect with nature at one of these escapes among the trees. Rejuvenate at a wellness retreat and spa in the Byron Bay hinterland or a hideaway in the foothills of the Blue Mountains. Discover a tropical treetop lodge in the Daintree Rainforest or a hotel in Victoria's Grampians National Park. Whichever path you choose, organic, farm-to-table produce is the order of the day.

Gaia Retreat & Spa

Surrender to the beauty and healing culture at this internationally awarded retreat. Set in the majestic Byron Bay Bundjalung Country hinterland, known as "the healing heartland of Australia", this retreat is perfectly positioned as a wellness sanctuary.

Nestled in 20 acres of breathtaking land on the easternmost point of Australia, Gaia Retreat & Spa is dedicated to honouring the spirit of Mother Earth. From the birds in the flowering gardens to the eco-conscious design, Gaia evokes a sense of peacefulness, tranquility and belonging. Co-founded in 2005 by Olivia Newton-John, Gaia offers bespoke holistic wellness programs aligned with its philosophy of gratitude, respect, organic and wellness. "When I first stood on this incredible land, it was so powerful. I refer to it as my barefoot meets Armani," says Newton-John.

At the heart of the Gaia experience lies its award-winning Day Spa with 10 treatment rooms and more than 35 healers and therapists. An extensive spa menu of therapeutic and restorative treatments will leave harried guests relaxed, revitalised and pampered. Drawing on holistic principles, Gaia has developed bespoke treatments, fitness and health programs, as well as alternative targeted therapies for both men and women. Gaia's wellness facilities include an outdoor heated saltwater pool, sauna, hot tub, steam room, yoga studio, fitness centre, tennis court and naturopathic consulting.

Accommodation consists of five styles of suites and villas from the classic Layana Room to the deluxe two-bedroom Komala Luxe Villa with its separate living area, fireplace and sweeping views of the hinterland.

Gaia's award-winning cuisine features a daily changing menu with a focus on paddock-to-plate offerings based on seasonal produce hand-picked straight from Gaia's organic gardens and small orchards, as well as sustainable, organic produce from local farmers and providores.

The retreat's all-inclusive breakfast, lunch and dinner menus are served at Kukura House (kukura means people in Sanskrit). Lunch may feature penne with roast pumpkin, radicchio, zucchini and preserved lemon or prawns with green mango, papaya, lime and herb salad. The three-course dinner may include prawn and pea risotto, steamed red emperor fillet with pumpkin, edamame, seaweed and dashi broth and passionfruit panna cotta with pineapple, lychee and mango salsa. Gaia offers a carefully curated wine list including some of the finest organic wines in Australia.

Gaia provides guests with a private space to realign themselves physically, spiritually and emotionally. With eight signature packages, guests can choose to stay for a few days or a week, to fully immerse themselves in this magical hinterland oasis. With restorative daily yoga, fun and inspiring activities to opt in or out of, along with rejuvenating spa treatments, all you need to do is surrender.

EXPLORE

• Watch the sun set over the Nightcap Range in Bundjalung Country from one of the Samira Lookout daybeds.

• Relax by the fire and take in the sweeping views of the hinterland, one of Olivia Newton-John's favourite spots for peaceful reflection.

Slow-roasted chicken leg, purple vegetables and fruits, hazelnuts

SERVES 4 // PREP TIME 30 MINS (PLUS CURING) // COOK 6 HRS (PLUS COOLING)

4   chicken Maryland (300gm each)
750   ml extra-virgin olive oil
750   ml melted duck fat
     Freeze-dried Davidson's plum powder
     (see note), baby amaranth leaves,
     Pedro Ximénez sherry vinegar,
     roasted hazelnuts and hazelnut oil,
     to serve

CURE
160   gm rock salt
110   gm rapadura sugar or brown sugar
5   thyme sprigs
2   bay leaves
2   garlic cloves
     Thinly peeled rind of 1 orange
½   tsp each juniper berries, coriander
     seeds, fennel seeds and black
     peppercorns

SAUCE
1   kg chicken wings, jointed
1   each celery stalk, carrot and brown
     onion, coarsely chopped
1   garlic head, halved horizontally
     Extra-virgin olive oil, for drizzling
200   ml dry white wine
10   thyme sprigs
4   fresh lemon myrtle leaves (see note)
3   fresh bay leaves
¼   tsp each coriander seeds, juniper
     berries and fennel seeds
10   black peppercorns
8   pepperberries, crushed (see note)
750   ml chicken stock

VEGETABLES
5   purple carrots (1kg), peeled, 4 halved
     lengthways, 1 thinly sliced on
     a mandolin
     Extra-virgin olive oil, for drizzling
4   beetroots (600gm), peeled
65   ml apple cider vinegar, plus extra,
     to taste
135   ml verjuice, plus extra, to taste
2   small golden shallots, thinly sliced
125   gm blackberries, halved
     Ground pepperberry, to taste
1   small radicchio, leaves separated,
     charred on an open flame on the
     stovetop

1 For cure, place ingredients in a food processor and pulse until finely chopped and combined. Place cure in a non-reactive container with chicken and toss well to coat. Position chicken so it is covered with the cure. Cover and refrigerate for a minimum of 8 hours or a maximum of 18 hours. Rinse cure from chicken then pat dry with paper towel.

2 For sauce, preheat oven to 240°C. Place chicken wings, vegetables and garlic in a large flame-proof roasting pan, drizzle with olive oil and toss to combine. Roast, stirring occasionally, until wings are golden and vegetables are caramelised (40-45 minutes).

3 Transfer roasted mixture to a large heavy-based 4-litre stockpot, scraping down pan to remove all browned bits. Place roasting pan over medium-high heat. Deglaze with wine, herbs and spices, and simmer until syrupy (1-2 minutes). Pour wine mixture over chicken wing and vegetable mixture. Add stock and approximately 500ml water to ensure ingredients are just submerged. Place stockpot over high heat and bring to a simmer. Reduce heat to low and simmer gently, skimming any impurities that rise to the surface and until reduced to a thin sauce (2½ hours). Remove from heat and stand on a wire rack for 30 minutes to infuse, then strain through a fine sieve into a small saucepan. Place pan over medium-high heat and simmer until reduced by half.

4 To cook chicken, preheat oven to 140°C. Place chicken in a flameproof roasting pan just large enough to fit chicken pieces. Pour over olive oil and duck fat. Place the pan over a medium heat and bring oil to a gentle simmer. Remove from heat, place a sheet of baking paper across the top then enclose roasting pan in foil. Transfer chicken to the oven and cook until very tender (2½ hours). Transfer roasting pan to a wire rack and keep warm until ready to serve. Alternatively you can make the recipe ahead and store under oil for up to 3 days refrigerated, then reheat as desired.

5 For vegetables, increase oven to 200°C. Place four halved carrots on an oven tray and drizzle with oil, season and roast until cooked (25 minutes). Meanwhile, place beetroot in a large saucepan, cover with 1 litre water and stir in 60ml vinegar and 125ml verjuice and season to taste. Bring to the boil over high heat. Reduce heat to medium and simmer until cooked (45 minutes). Drain and reserve 150ml poaching liquid. Transfer beetroot and reserved poaching liquid to a blender and blend to a purée, adjust flavour with extra verjuice and vinegar to taste; season. Makes 375ml. Set aside and keep warm until required.

6 Place shallots, blackberries and sliced carrot in a small bowl with remaining 2 tsp verjuice, 1 tsp vinegar and a pinch of pepperberry; season with salt and toss to combine.

7 To finish and sear chicken, remove chicken from oil and drain on paper towel. Heat a large non-stick frying pan with 2cm of the chicken cooking oil, avoiding any cooking juices. Cook chicken (take care of the splashing oil) skin-side down until golden (2-3 minutes), turn and cook further until golden and chicken is heated through (3 minutes).

8 To serve, place chicken on one half of each plate, then spoon small spoonfuls of beetroot purée on the other side. Arrange pickled carrot mixture, a roasted carrot, charred torn radicchio leaves around purée then spoon over sauce. Scatter with roasted hazelnuts and baby amaranth. Drizzle with Pedro Ximénez sherry vinegar and hazelnut oil. Sprinkle with Davidson's plum powder and extra ground pepperberry.

NOTE Davidson's plum powder, lemon myrtle leaves and pepperberry are available online from native-food specialist stores. Pedro Ximénez sherry vinegar has a mahogany colour and sweet flavour. If it's unavailable, substitute vincotto. Leftover oil can be ladled from the dish (avoiding cooking juices on the base) and used to repeat the recipe. Keep refrigerated for up to 1 month.

PREPARE AHEAD Sauce and slow-roasted chicken can be made a day ahead.

WINE MATCH 2020 De Bortoli The Estate Gamay, Yarra Valley, Vic.

Passionfruit white chocolate parfait, banana, yuzu and coconut

SERVES 6 // PREP TIME 35 MINS (PLUS FREEZING, CHILLING) // COOK 1 HR 45 MINS (PLUS COOLING)

"This dessert isn't our typical retreat style due to the inclusion of white chocolate," says head chef Dan Trewartha. "As a wholefoods-based kitchen, we don't use refined sugars. Our desserts are gluten-free, dairy-free and vegan." Begin this recipe a day ahead.

Banana, grated white chocolate, micro lemon balm leaves, to serve

PARFAIT
180 gm white organic chocolate, finely chopped
80 ml coconut cream
100 ml passionfruit juice (7 passionfruit; see note)
5 egg yolks
60 gm coconut sugar
420 gm non-dairy coconut yoghurt
¼ tsp xanthan gum (see note)
Sea salt flakes

ROASTED BANANA PURÉE
3 bananas (400gm), unpeeled
1½ tbsp raw honey
60 ml unroasted macadamia butter (see note)
1½ tsp yuzu juice

PASSIONFRUIT SYRUP
160 ml passionfruit juice (11 large passionfruit; see note)
1 tbsp coconut syrup, or to taste
1 tbsp yuzu juice, or to taste
⅛ tsp xanthan gum (see note)

COCONUT CHIPS
15 gm eggwhite
1 tbsp coconut sugar
1 tsp yuzu juice, or to taste
50 gm coconut flakes

1 For parfait, stir 100gm of the white chocolate and the coconut cream in a small saucepan over medium heat until chocolate melts (2 minutes). Transfer to a bowl and cool in the fridge, stirring occasionally. Once cool, stir in passionfruit juice. Place egg yolks and coconut sugar in a large heatproof bowl over a saucepan of simmering water. Whisk continuously until pale and thick (3-4 minutes). Transfer mixture to an electric mixer fitted with a whisk attachment and whisk on high speed until tripled in volume (5 minutes). Meanwhile, whisk coconut yoghurt and xanthan gum by hand in a bowl until thickened slightly (4 minutes). Fold cooled white chocolate mixture into whipped coconut yoghurt, then fold combined coconut mixture into the whipped egg yolks. Spoon mixture into individual 125ml half-sphere silicon moulds (or a 10cm x 24cm lined loaf tin). Makes 720gm. Freeze for 5 hours or overnight until set.

2 For roasted banana purée, preheat oven to 160°C. Place unpeeled bananas on an oven tray and roast until soft and tender (15 minutes). Peel and place in a high-speed blender with remaining ingredients and blend until puréed (1 minute). Transfer to a container, cover directly with plastic wrap and cool completely. Makes 350ml. Refrigerate until required.

3 For passionfruit syrup, place ingredients in a large bowl and whisk to combine. Adjust syrup flavour if necessary with more syrup or yuzu juice for a tangy syrup to cut through the richness of the parfait. Makes 200ml.

4 For coconut chips, preheat oven to 160°C and line a large oven tray with baking paper. Combine eggwhite, sugar and yuzu in a bowl. Add coconut and toss gently to coat. Place on prepared tray. Roast, stirring occasionally, or until golden (25 minutes). Cool then store in an airtight container until required.

5 For caramelised white chocolate, reduce oven 140°C. Grease and line an oven tray with baking paper. Scatter remaining 80gm white chocolate over prepared tray and scatter with sea salt flakes. Roast, stirring every 15 minutes with a silicon spatula, or until golden and caramelised (1 hour). Cool. Store in an airtight container until required.

6 To serve, unmould parfaits and place on plates with 2 quenelles of banana purée. Scatter with grated white chocolate, sliced bananas, caramelised white chocolate and coconut chips. Spoon some passionfruit syrup into the centre of the plate. Top with banana pieces and micro lemon balm leaves.

NOTE Xanthan gum is used as a thickener. Unroasted macadamia butter, available from health-food stores, is used as a dairy replacement due to its neutral flavour that gives dishes a fat content, and thickens and stabilises creams and purées. To obtain passionfruit juice, process passionfruit pulp, then push mixture through a fine sieve and discard seeds.

PREPARE AHEAD Parfait, passionfruit syrup and coconut chips can be made a day ahead.

WINE MATCH 2020 Vasse Felix Cane Cut Semillion, Margaret River, WA.

Spicers Sangoma Retreat

A tranquil escape awaits at this exclusive bushland retreat in the foothills of the Blue Mountains with farm-to-table dining, restorative spa experiences and luxury lodgings.

At the foothills of the Blue Mountains National Park stands Spicers Sangoma Retreat, an adults-only all-inclusive sanctuary with its eight intimate suites the epitome of Australian bush luxury. Living up to its Zulu name for healer, Sangoma offers guests a place to unwind and rejuvenate with its serene seclusion, seasonal dining and restorative spa experiences just over an hour's drive from Sydney.

The original African-style lodgings designed by Sydney architect, Barbara Tarnawski, underwent a makeover in 2016 in consultation with the Spicers design team. Designed to blend seamlessly with the bushland surrounds, the interiors team natural timber accents with soft furnishings in a warm palette of stone, ecru and earthy brown. Each suite includes a custom-built king-size bed, ensuite, fireplace, bath/rainshower, underfloor heating and wraparound verandah.

The premium Chief Suite spans two levels with panoramic views of the bush and the Sydney city skyline on a clear day. Separate living, dining and kitchen areas downstairs with a wood-burning fireplace and private heated plunge pool and deck offer the ultimate place to unwind and reconnect with nature.

For a truly unique experience that is sure to immerse you in the sights and sounds of the Australian bush, check in to the Tent Suite. Positioned so that it feels like it's in the middle of the bush in a lofty safari tent-style suite with timber floors, overhead crystal chandelier and open-plan bathroom with freestanding Philippe Starck bath, this is as close to living in the treetops as you'll get.

The African theme pervades Sangoma's Spa Anise treatments; knead away stress with the restorative dovadova therapy or amatshe stone massage or rejuvenate with the perfumed amakatherapy which uses essential oils and massage to relax the body. The spa offers nine signature treatments designed to let you disconnect and recharge in the tranquil bushland setting. Take your relaxation to the next level with a personal yoga or meditation class.

The kitchen team at Sangoma's restaurant Amara (West African for grace) offers diners a "chef's harvest experience" with dishes made from organic, seasonal produce from the Hawkesbury region's Harvest Farms project. A five-course dégustation lunch includes plant-forward dishes such as beetroot, burnt vegetable jus and horseradish snow. Flavoursome confit squid, salted daikon and onion broth and roasted chicken, celeriac, onion relish and radish leaf amp up the protein in the seven-course dinner menu which is a truly graceful dining experience that's recently opened to outside guests.

EXPLORE

• Be inspired by the natural surrounds to create your own artwork at the Wine and Watercolours art class.

• Follow farm-gate trails to distilleries, wineries and orchards to discover all the local produce for your next feast.

Smoked pork loin, caramelised garlic, pickled grapes and chamomile

SERVES 6 // PREP TIME 25 MINS (PLUS DRYING, PICKLING, COOLING) // COOK 7 HRS 20 MINS (PLUS RESTING)

"It is always good to use free-range, and if possible, organic meats and produce, as we do in this dish using pork from Melanda Park farm in New South Wales," says head chef Will Houia. You will need to start the recipe 1-2 days ahead to dry the pork skin.

1	kg pork loin, bone-in
2	tbsp vegetable oil, plus extra, for drizzling and brushing
1	carrot, diced
1	onion, diced
1	celery stalk, diced
4	garlic cloves
6	black peppercorns
10	juniper berries
500	ml red wine
4	litres water
2	bay leaves
200	gm applewood smoking chips
1	tsp dried chamomile tea
12	baby cos lettuce leaves

PICKLED GRAPES

2	tsp fennel seeds
2	tsp coriander seeds
100	gm caster sugar
100	ml water
75	ml white wine vinegar
150	gm green grapes, halved

CARAMELISED GARLIC EMULSION

500	gm peeled raw garlic
185	ml cane cut semilion (dessert wine)
200	ml pouring cream

1 To dry pork skin, 1-2 days ahead, place pork, skin-side up, on a tray lined with paper towel then refrigerate uncovered.

2 For pickled grapes, dry-roast seeds in a small frying pan over medium heat until fragrant (2 minutes). Cool. Place seeds, sugar, water and vinegar in a saucepan, bring to the boil then set aside to cool. Place grapes in a jar and cover with pickling liquid. Refrigerate for at least 1 day.

3 To remove pork skin, carefully run a knife under the skin, then remove the bone of the loin and break down the bones into smaller pieces (or have your butcher do this).

4 Preheat oven to 200°C. Place bones on an oven tray and roast until dark (45 minutes). Heat 1 tbsp oil in a stockpot over medium heat. Add vegetables, garlic, peppercorns and juniper and cook, stirring until lightly browned (8 minutes). Add wine and simmer until reduced by one-third (8-10 minutes). Add browned bones, the water and bay then bring to the boil. Reduce heat to low-medium and cook, skimming the top occasionally, or until liquid is reduced by three-quarters (6 minutes). Strain stock into a small saucepan. You should have 1 litre. Continue simmering and skimming over medium heat until reduced by three-quarters to a thick jus (15-20 minutes).

5 Preheat oven to 180°C. Trim pork skin into an even square or rectangle shape. Cut into 1cm-wide strips and place on an oven tray lined with baking paper. Brush with 1 tbsp oil and sprinkle with salt. Cover with a second sheet of baking paper and weigh down with a second heavy oven tray. Bake until skin is crackled (1¼ hours). Brush crackling with extra oil then push chamomile through a fine sieve over crackling.

6 Bring pork to room temperature (2 hours). Preheat oven to 120°C. Make sure that the kitchen is well ventilated as there will be a lot smoke. Sear pork loin in a frying pan over medium-high heat on all sides until golden. Transfer to a wire rack. Place smoking chips on an oven tray then place a wire tray over the top. Light the chips with a high-powered blow torch until they produce heavy smoke. Quickly place on the bottom of the oven and place pork on an upper oven shelf to turn your oven into a smoking chamber. Smoke for 30 minutes, re-lighting the chips if they go out, or until pork is a darkish brown. Reduce oven to 70°C and continue smoking pork until an internal temperatue of between 65-69°C is reached (1½ hours). Rest pork for 15 minutes.

7 Meanwhile, for caramelised garlic emulsion, blanch garlic in boiling water 3 times and drain. Place garlic in a large heavy-based frying pan with dessert wine and simmer over medium heat until caramelised (3-4 minutes). Add cream and reduce until almost evaporated (2 minutes). Transfer mixture to a high-speed blender and blend until smooth. Refrigerate until required.

8 Carve pork into six 1.5cm-thick slices. Gently reheat garlic emulsion in a small saucepan, stirring to avoid lumps (add water if it gets lumpy). Gently warm drained pickled grapes in pork jus in a second small pan. Heat a heavy-based frying pan over high heat. Brush cos leaves with oil and cook briefly on one side until edge is charred.

9 To serve, divide pork among plates, place a strip of pork skin, pickled grapes and jus over the pork and a spoonful of garlic emulsion to one side. Finish with the cos lettuce filling the other side of the plate.

PREPARE AHEAD Jus, pickled grapes and caramelised garlic emulsion can be made a day ahead.

WINE MATCH 2019 Moorilla Praxis Chardonnay Musqué, Berriedale, Tas.

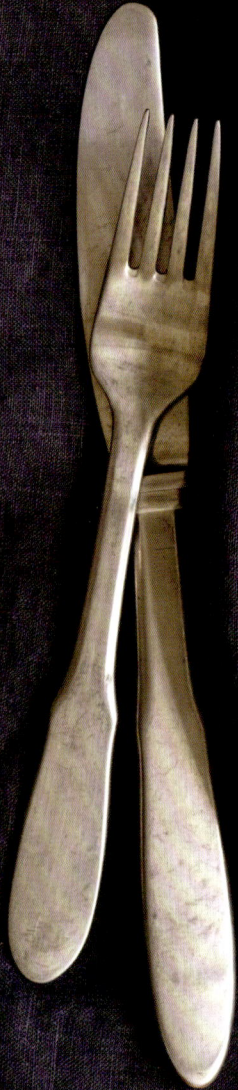

Braised lamb shoulder, broccoli and broad beans

SERVES 6 // PREP TIME 30 MINS (PLUS COOLING) // COOK 6 HRS 40 MINS

"We source our lamb for this recipe from the lush green pastures of Cowra in New South Wales," says Houia. "To honour good produce such as this we treat it simply, yet the end result is delicious and decadent, perfect to impress any guest."

1 kg fresh unpodded broad beans (or 500gm defrosted frozen broad beans)
1 tbsp olive oil
1 cup small mint leaves

BRAISED LAMB SHOULDER
2 kg whole lamb shoulder
1 onion, cut into wedges
2 celery stalks, coarsely chopped
1 tsp coriander seeds
¾ tsp caraway seeds
3 star anise
½ tsp black peppercorns
1 tsp cloves
2 tomatoes, diced
3 garlic cloves, bruised
6 thyme sprigs
3 flat-leaf parsley sprigs
200 ml red wine

BROCCOLI PURÉE
2 tsp caraway seeds
250 gm broccoli (1 head)
200 gm baby spinach leaves
150 ml chilled water
1 tbsp lemon juice

1 For braised lamb shoulder, heat oven to 240°C. Place lamb in a deep roasting pan and cook until browned (45 minutes). Add onion and celery and cook for a further 5 minutes. Add the remaining ingredients and enough water to reach three-quarters of the way up the side of the lamb. Cover the top of the lamb with a sheet of baking paper, then cover the dish tightly with foil. Reduce oven to 150°C and continue cooking until the lamb is very tender and the meat is falling from the bone (4½-5 hours).

2 Cool lamb in braising liquid (1 hour), then remove and strain braising liquid through a fine sieve into a heavy-based saucepan. Cool the braising liquid in the fridge until the fat solidifies on the top (1½ hours). Discard the fat, then simmer the saucepan of braising liquid over medium heat until reduced to a thin jus (45-50 minutes). Strain through a fine sieve and refrigerate until required.

3 Carefully remove all bones from the lamb shoulder while trying to keep it whole as much as possible. Lay out two large squares of plastic wrap on a bench, large enough to place the lamb on. Place the lamb meat on the plastic wrap, flattening it to create an even shape, similar to how you would shape sushi rice, then like making sushi, using the plastic wrap, roll up the lamb as tight as possible to form a tight cylinder. Continue to tighten, twisting the excess plastic wrap at each end until the meat forms a roulade shape. (Make sure to push ends in and tighten and tie as hard as possible so the lamb is very compact.) Refrigerate rolled lamb until set (3 hours) or until required.

4 For broccoli purée, bring a large saucepan of water to the boil. Fill a bowl with ice and water. Place caraway seeds in a small frying pan and dry-roast until fragrant (1 minute). Cool. Quarter broccoli head. Blanch in the boiling water until tender (3-4 minutes). Remove with a slotted spoon and refresh in iced water (reserve boiling water). Drain. Transfer broccoli to a high-speed blender with caraway seeds, spinach and chilled water and blend on high until smooth (2 minutes). Strain through a fine sieve into a bowl. Season with lemon juice and salt. Refrigerate until required. Makes 750ml.

5 For broad beans, remove beans from the pod, then blanch in reserved boiling water (30 seconds), drain and refesh in iced water. Drain again, then peel skins from beans.

6 Fifteen minutes before serving, preheat oven to 180°C. Cut lamb into 6 portions (about 200gm each). Heat olive oil in a large frying pan over medium-high heat. Cook lamb, turning until golden all over (5-6 minutes). Transfer to an oven tray lined with baking paper and cook until heated through (10 minutes).

7 To serve, heat jus, broccoli purée and broad beans on a low heat until just warmed. Place lamb on the plate, then broccoli mixture and broad beans to the side, scattered with mint leaves. Spoon lamb jus generously over lamb.

PREPARE AHEAD Lamb and jus can be made up until the end of step 3 a day ahead.

WINE MATCH 2017 Leeuwin Estate Art Series Cabernet Sauvignon, Margaret River, WA.

Silky Oaks Lodge

Experience the ultimate in luxury rainforest resorts at this unique treetop escape on the banks of Queensland's Mossman River.

Tucked away between the ancient rainforest and iconic sugarcane fields of Tropical North Queensland, Silky Oaks Lodge sits on some of the area's most prized real estate. Nestled on the banks of the Mossman River, this beautiful retreat is just a short drive to the world-famous Daintree Rainforest and the beaches of nearby Port Douglas and Cooya Beach.

A visit to Silky Oaks Lodge offers guests the opportunity to lose themselves in the beauty of the World Heritage-listed Daintree Rainforest and relax in a contemporary, treehouse-inspired lodge. With jungle perch, turtles and platypus in the river below and bright-blue Ulysses butterflies and an abundance of native birds in the treetops, the sights and sounds of the forest envelope guests in an extraordinary natural theatre.

One of the lodge's six new suite categories, the Daintree Pavilion, sets the benchmark for tropical luxury with its dramatic skillion ceilings held aloft by glass walls, Australian furniture and tiered infinity pool and plunge spa floating among the cool of the forest. All suites offer a unique sense of the region with custom finishes, commisioned artworks and private decks to take in rainforest or river views.

The recently renovated Treehouse Restaurant blends the classic Queensland vernacular with a cool and contemporary vibe. Nestled among the treetops at birds' nest height, the dining space is enveloped by old mango trees and other native flora.

The kitchen's ingredients come direct from the surrounding rainforest and nearby Atherton Tablelands, which both offer a plentiful supply of biodynamic and organic produce. Native fruit, local meat, sustainably sourced seafood and other ingredients are delivered daily to the restaurant by farmers and suppliers within a small radius of Silky Oaks Lodge. The team relies on this bounty of local produce to create a refined modern Australian menu with an Asian twist. Dishes take shape around local fresh produce such as Daintree barramundi, kangaroo or king cobia.

Try the red claw sour curry with Malaysian lime or char siu pork belly wonton soup with chilli, bitter melon and prawn oil. For dessert, there's a coconut mousse with persimmon, lemon verbena and chocolate. All courses are matched with premium drops from Australian winemakers.

Whether you enjoy a safari tour, a hike along rainforest tracks, a dip in the swimming holes or a pampering treatment at the Healing Waters Spa, these are just a few of the ways to experience the magic of the Daintree.

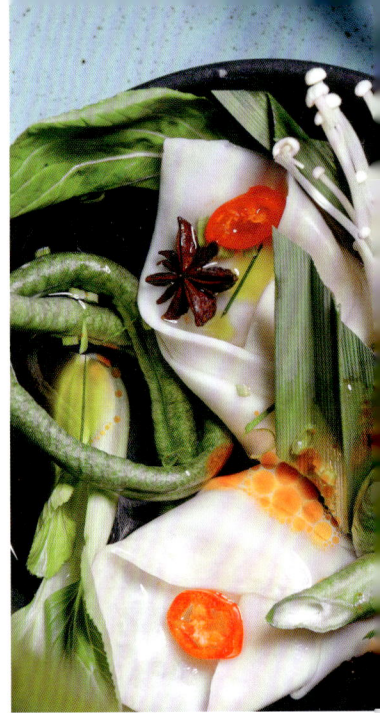

EXPLORE

• Enjoy a *Jungle Book* vibe with a chef's table experience under the rainforest canopy among the property's kitchen garden.

• Immerse yourself in the sights and sounds of the rainforest with a hike along the Fig Tree Rapids trail. Take a refreshing dip in the freshwater billabong along the way.

Grilled shio koji salmon with edamame salad and sesame dressing

SERVES 4 // PREP TIME 45 MINS (PLUS 7 DAYS FERMENTING, OVERNIGHT MARINATING) // COOK 30 MINS

"By marinating salmon in shio koji, the salmon's proteins are broken down and converted into umami (sugar and glutamic acids). The simple salad keeps the salmon the star," says executive chef Mark Godbeer. Ferment the shio koji for this recipe 8 days ahead.

Black sesame seeds and baby mizuna, to serve

SHIO KOJI
105 gm koji rice, ground to a powder (see note)
160 ml water
2½ tsp kosher salt (or iodine-free salt)

EDAMAME SALAD
1 tbsp soy sauce
60 ml rice wine vinegar
1 tsp fish sauce
¾ tsp fine sea salt
2 tbsp avocado or extra-virgin olive oil
1 cup frozen podded edamame, steamed, refreshed
8 red radishes, cut into julienne
½ Lebanese cucumber, seeds removed, diced
3 spring onions, thinly sliced
⅓ cup round mint leaves, thinly sliced
2 tbsp thinly sliced coriander
1 tbsp lime zest

SESAME DRESSING
1 long red chilli, coarsely chopped
80 ml roasted sesame oil
40 gm sesame seeds, toasted
95 gm coconut yoghurt or Japanese mayonnaise
80 ml rice wine vinegar
60 ml soy sauce
2 tbsp mirin

SHIO KOJI SALMON
120 gm shio koji
1 tbsp gochujang (Korean chilli paste, see note)
80 ml soy sauce
1 tsp rice wine vinegar
1 tbsp finely chopped lemongrass
1 tbsp finely grated ginger
1 tbsp finely chopped garlic
4 pieces skinless salmon fillets (3cm thick), pin-boned, belly trimmed
2 tbsp coconut oil, melted

1 For shio koji, stir ingredients in a bowl until well combined; mixture will resemble runny porridge. Transfer to a glass jar and seal. Store in a place with an ambient temperature greater than 20°C and stir once a day for a week. After day 4 the mixture with start to develop a progressive fermented flavour. On day 8 refrigerate shio until required or for for up to 6 months.

2 For edamame salad, place soy sauce, vinegar, fish sauce and salt in a glass bowl and stir until salt dissolves. Whisk in avocado oil, then add remaining ingredients and toss gently to coat. Cover and refrigerate for the salt to extract moisture from ingredients and flavours to meld (1 hour).

3 For sesame dressing, place chilli in a heatproof bowl, cover with boiling water and stand 1 minute, then drain. Place chilli with remaining ingredients in a high-speed blender and blend until smooth (1-2 minutes). Pass through a fine sieve, pressing down with spatula. Season to taste, then transfer to a squeeze bottle until required.

4 For shio koji salmon, place ingredients, except salmon and oil, in a high-speed blender and blend for 30 seconds. Transfer mixture to a snap-lock bag and add salmon pieces, remove as much air as possible and seal the bag. Massage the koji mix through the bag to evenly distribute. Refrigerate for 12 hours, turning the bag after 6 hours.

5 Remove salmon from the bag and wipe off excess marinade. Lightly brush salmon with coconut oil (see note). Preheat a barbecue or char-grill pan to medium-high. Grill salmon for 1½-2 minutes each side for medium/medium-rare, or for medium/well done, for 3½-4 minutes each side. Set aside to rest for 2 minutes.

6 To serve, using a slotted spoon, spoon ¾ cup edamame salad into the centre of a shallow bowl. Slice salmon into 3 pieces and place over the salad. Top with baby mizuna. Squeeze 3-4 tbsp sesame dressing onto the plate and sprinkle with black sesame seeds.

NOTE Koji rice is steamed rice that has been inoculated with koji starter, a mould that releases enzymes that ferment the rice. Koji and gochujang are available from Japanese and Asian grocers. Keep an eye on the salmon once it's on the grill as the shio koji will break down the salmon proteins, resulting in a higher sugar content and quicker browning effect.

PREPARE AHEAD Shio koji must be prepared at least 8 days ahead. Sesame dressing can be made a day ahead.

WINE MATCH 2019 Montalto Estate Pinot Gris, Mornington Peninsula, Vic.

Miso caramel trout in chilli soy broth

SERVES 4 // PREP TIME 40 MINS (PLUS INFUSING) // COOK 35 MINS

"This is a very straightforward dish, creating the quick (yet punchy) broth in the same pan that you cook the coral trout in," says Godbeer. "The Asian vegetables bring balance to the naturally sweet coral trout and aromatic broth."

4   **coral trout fillets (150gm each)**
    Sesame oil, for cooking
    Lime cheeks, to serve

MISO CARAMEL
1   **star anise**
4   **cm piece galangal or ginger, peeled, halved**
60   **ml water**
1   **makrut lime leaf**
80   **gm panela or caster sugar (see note)**
1   **tbsp fish sauce**
2   **tbsp shiro (white) miso**
1   **tbsp each lime and orange juice**

JULIENNE VEGETABLE SALAD
2   **large broccoli stems/hearts (see note)**
100   **gm snow peas**
5   **spring onions**
400   **gm small daikon**
1   **small fennel bulb (150gm)**

CHILLI SOY BROTH
2   **tbsp ghee**
3   **garlic cloves, thinly sliced**
2   **long red chillies, thinly sliced**
½   **cup coriander roots and stems**
2   **makrut lime leaves, centre vein removed, thinly sliced**
60   **ml lemon juice**
60   **ml soy sauce**
500   **ml chicken stock**
1   **tsp katsuobushi (see note)**

1 For miso caramel, place star anise, galangal, water and lime leaf in a heavy-based saucepan. Bring to the boil then remove from heat, cover with a lid and set aside to infuse (30 minutes). Remove spices and lime leaf then return saucepan to medium heat. Add sugar and stir without boiling until sugar dissolves. Increase heat to medium-high and simmer, without stirring until a dark golden caramel forms (8 minutes). Remove from heat. Taking care as the mixture will splutter, add fish sauce, miso, lime and orange juices and stir until well combined. Set aside until required.

2 For julienne vegetable salad, trim vegetables into 5cm slices, then cut into julienne so each vegetable is cut into 5cm strips. (Cut to this size they will soften slightly with the heat of the broth but still retain some crunch.) Combine julienne vegetables in a bowl. Refrigerate until required.

3 For fish, preheat oven to 180°C. Heat a heavy-based ovenproof frying pan over high heat. Brush trout fillets with sesame oil and season. Sear trout for 1 minute each side or until well-coloured. Liberally brush trout with miso caramel. Transfer to the oven and roast, brushing with a thin layer of miso caramel halfway through cooking time or until just cooked through (5-7 minutes). Transfer trout to a tray and keep warm. Reserve frying pan.

4 For chilli soy broth, return reserved pan to a medium-high heat, add ghee and stir with a wooden spoon to deglaze pan (30 seconds). Add garlic, chilli, coriander and lime leaves and cook stirring until garlic is just golden (1 minute), taking care not to burn it or the broth will be bitter. Add remaining ingredients and bring to the boil, then reduce to a gentle simmer until trout is ready to plate. Check seasoning and acid are balanced.

5 To serve, divide julienne vegetables among bowls and place a piece of coral trout on top. Spoon the chilli and garlic slices from the broth over the fish then divide the broth among bowls. Serve with lime cheeks.

NOTE Panela sugar is produced mainly in Colombia, where it's usually sold in block form; in Australia, it's more often seen as a granulated product. For broccoli heart, trim florets from 2 heads of broccoli and reserve for another use; trim remaining stems straight in preparation to julienne. Katsuobushi, dried bonito flakes, are available from Japanese grocers.

PREPARE AHEAD Chilli soy broth can be made a day ahead.

WINE MATCH 2018 Audrey Wilkinson Tempranillo, Hunter Valley, NSW.

Royal Mail Hotel

This hotel at the edge of the Grampians National Park offers an epicurean haven with farm-to-table dining, a bountiful kitchen garden and an impressive wine cellar to match.

Located at the southern tip of the spectacular Grampians National Park in Dunkeld, the Royal Mail Hotel offers a one-of-a-kind experience with award-winning dining, boutique accommodation and a selection of food, wine and nature-based experiences.

Accommodation includes a range of deluxe suites as well as cottage stays at nearby Mt Sturgeon Station. Hotel guest rooms offer private balconies with picturesque views overlooking native gardens and the Southern Grampians. Mt Sturgeon Station guests can stay at the grand six-bedroom Homestead or the one- or two-bedroom Mt Sturgeon Cottages and enjoy full access and transfers to the Royal Mail Hotel for dining and facilities.

Two restaurants, led by British-born executive chef Robin Wickens (ex-Interlude, Melbourne), reveal his passion for hyper-local dining with dishes conjured from the hotel's 1.2-hectare kitchen garden, the largest of its kind in the southern hemisphere. Wickens at Royal Mail Hotel is the chef's most personal project with beef and lamb dishes from the hotel's farm as well as produce from its kitchen garden.

The dining experience at Wickens at Royal Mail Hotel is crafted around the hotel's four stories – food, wine, people and place. The fine-diner's dégustation menu can include Royal Mail lamb, brassicas and nettle sauce, smoked Great Ocean duck, Jerusalem artichoke, maple and pine. There is also a daily changing vegetarian menu.

The casual Parker Street Project offers à la carte lunch and dinner menus with seasonal dishes that show off produce from the kitchen garden, orchards, greenhouses and olive groves. Seafood, poultry, game and pork are sourced from nearby suppliers to complement the sustainably driven menus.

The daily Kitchen Garden Tour conducted by the hotel's chefs and gardeners demonstrate the organic practices employed by the hotel and how the daily harvest influences the menu. The wine cellar houses one of the most comprehensive and varied wine collections in Australia with 30,000 bottles. The Royal Mail Hotel Cellar Tour offers guests the opportunity to journey through the hotel's wine collection and enjoy a sommelier-led comparative tasting of local and international wines.

The hotel's conservation department's captive breeding program aims to increase numbers of threatened species such as eastern quolls, fat-tailed dunnarts and sugar gliders. Guests can join a guided native wildlife tour during feeding times each day of the week. Private walks to discover local wildlife, native flora and fauna, and wildflowers are also available for guests to enjoy.

EXPLORE

• Go behind the scenes with a tour and tasting in the Royal Mail's award-winning wine cellar that houses 30,000 bottles of the finest wines and rare finds, including both local and international labels.

• Hike the nearby Grampians Peaks Trail with an eco-guide and discover Aboriginal rock art sites, native birdlife and beautiful waterfalls.

Great Ocean duck, celery custard, rhubarb and spinach

SERVES 8 // PREP TIME 35 MINS (PLUS BRINING) // COOK 3 HRS 15 MINS (PLUS COOLING, RESTING)

"This is an adaptation of my recipe, using celery for angelica, red rhubarb for green, and English spinach for Malabar spinach," says executive chef Robin Wickens. "I dry-age the ducks for 3 weeks to develop the flavour. We make duck meatloaf from the Marylands."

3 kg duck
2 tsp grapeseed oil
250 gm large-leaf English spinach

DUCK AND RHUBARB SAUCE
1 tbsp grapeseed oil
1 each carrot, celery stalk, onion, leek, coarsely chopped
150 ml red wine
600 ml gelatinous chicken stock
500 ml veal stock
1 stalk rhubarb, chopped

RHUBARB PURÉE
200 ml water
150 gm caster sugar
200 gm rhubarb, cut into 5cm lengths
2½ tbsp lemon juice

RHUBARB GLAZE
140 gm caster sugar
50 ml red wine vinegar
140 ml fresh rhubarb juice (see note)

CELERY CUSTARD
600 ml milk
100 ml pouring cream
150 gm celery leaves and stalks, chopped
3 eggs

1 Separate duck into Marylands, wings, neck and remove the backbone. You will be left with the crown – breasts attached to the rib cage. Brine crown if you want (see cook's notes, p222). Reserve Marylands for another recipe.

2 For duck and rhubarb sauce, heat oil in a large saucepan over medium-high heat. Sauté vegetables until golden (8 minutes). Add wine and reduce until syrupy. Add stocks, wings, neck and backbone. Bring to the boil, then reduce to low and simmer gently for 1½ hours. Strain sauce into a large clean frying pan. Simmer over medium heat until reduced by two-thirds (15 minutes). Refrigerate until required. Makes 1 cup.

3 For rhubarb purée, place water and sugar in a small saucepan. Bring to the boil, stirring to dissolve sugar. Add rhubarb and poach until soft (4 minutes). Cool slightly then strain the syrup from the rhubarb. Blend the rhubarb with a little strained syrup to a smooth purée consistency. (Reserve remaining syrup for another use). Season purée with salt and stir through 1-2 tbsp lemon juice for a sharp taste.

4 For rhubarb glaze, heat sugar in a heavy-based saucepan, swirling the pan, over medium-high heat until a dark caramel (3 minutes). Taking care as the mixture will splutter, add vinegar and bring to the boil, then add rhubarb juice. Bring to the boil, then boil until reduced by half (2 minutes). Set aside at room temperature.

5 For celery custard, warm milk and cream in a saucepan over low heat. Add chopped celery and gently simmer until softened (10 minutes). Transfer to a blender and blend until smooth and green. Pass mixture through a fine sieve. Adjust seasoning with fine salt and sugar if it is bitter. Skim the foam. Weigh 600gm of the celery mixture and whisk in eggs. Check seasoning again and adjust. Divide custard among eight 125ml plastic dariole moulds. Wrap each tightly with a piece of plastic wrap. Transfer to a steamer and steam over low heat until just set with a slight wobble (15-20 minutes). Set aside at room temperature until ready to serve.

6 Preheat oven to 220°C. Heat grapeseed oil in a large frying pan over medium heat. Brown duck crown, skin-side down, turning, for 5 minutes until golden and fat has rendered. Remove from the pan. Drain fat from pan and reserve 2 tsp for sautéeing spinach. Transfer duck to a lined oven tray and brush with some of the rhubarb glaze. Roast, glazing every 5 minutes, or until internal temperature of breast meats reaches 58°C (18-20 minutes). Remove from oven. Brush with extra glaze, cover loosely with foil and rest for 40 minutes.

7 Meanwhile, to finish duck and rhubarb sauce, bring jus to the boil in a small saucepan over medium heat. Add rhubarb and remove from heat and cover tightly with plastic wrap. Set aside to steep until ready to serve, then strain. Do not reboil at this stage.

8 Sauté spinach in reserved duck fat until wilted (1½ minutes). Season to taste.

9 To serve, carve duck breasts from the crown and slice each into 4 portions. Unmould a celery custard onto each plate. Place spinach leaves on the plate then the duck breast on top. Place a few spoonfuls of rhubarb purée around the duck and drizzle with duck sauce.

NOTE For rhubarb juice, process 375gm rhubarb until juices release, then press through a sieve. Makes 150ml.

WINE MATCH 2019 d'Arenberg The Feral Fox Pinot Noir, Adelaide Hills, SA.

Aged beef tartare, beet, oyster cream and oyster crackers

SERVES 8 // PREP TIME 1 HR 45 MINS (PLUS COOLING, INFUSING) // COOK 2 HRS (PLUS OVERNIGHT DEHYDRATING)

6 red beetroots (150gm each)
4 small golden beetroots (25gm each)
150 ml beetroot juice
15 gm fresh horseradish, peeled and coarsely chopped
⅛ tsp xanthan gum
700 gm dry-aged beef sirloin
1 tbsp ascorbic acid
100 ml cold water
60 ml extra-virgin olive oil
Chive flowers and red garnet amaranth

OYSTER CRACKERS
2 dozen Sydney Rock oysters, freshly shucked (120gm), juices reserved
120 gm tapioca flour
Vegetable oil, for deep-frying

OYSTER CREAM
250 ml pouring cream
1 dozen Sydney Rock oysters (60gm), freshly shucked, juices reserved
4 gm agar agar
2 egg yolks
1 tbsp caster sugar
¾ tsp fine salt
1¼ tsp cornflour

1 The day before serving, start on the oyster crackers. Blend shucked oysters and reserved juices in a blender to a smooth purée. Weigh purée and stir in 70 per cent of the same weight in tapioca flour to form a thick spreadable mixture the consistency of tahini. Spread one-quarter of the mixture between 2 sheets of baking paper, then using a rolling pin, press out the mixture until 1-2mm thick and 22cm round. Repeat three more times with remaining mixture and more baking paper. Place a three-tiered steamer over a saucepan of boiling water. Steam the sheets in a steamer (you need 4 layers – one for each cracker – a large bamboo steamer with multiple layers works best) for 45 minutes, then allow to cool in the fridge, ideally overnight. Peel mixture off the paper and transfer to a food dehydrator. Dehydrate at 60°C for 8-10 hours.

2 On the day of serving, preheat oven to 180°C. Layer a sheet of foil with baking paper. Place red beetroot on top and form into a parcel, place on oven tray and bake until tender (1 hour). Repeat process with golden beetroot; bake until tender (45 minutes).

3 Meanwhile, for oyster cream, bring cream to the boil in a small saucepan. Add oysters and reserved juices, remove the pan from heat, cover with plastic wrap and stand to infuse (20 minutes). Strain oyster cream through a fine sieve, pressing lightly to release the flavour from the oysters. Discard cooked oysters and weigh the cream. You need 400gm infused cream. Depending on how juicy the oysters are, you may have more or less. Discard any excess cream. If short, add a little cream to make up the weight. Place infused cream in a clean saucepan with remaining ingredients. Whisk over medium heat until mixture boils and thickens (1 minute). Transfer to a container, cover directly with plastic wrap and refrigerate until set. Blend cream in a blender until smooth and thick. (If mixture splits continue blending with a little water until combined).

4 Combine beetroot juice and horseradish in a small saucepan and heat to 60°C (7-8 minutes); do not boil. Remove from heat and cover and steep (2 hours).

5 Meanwhile, for beef tartare, remove any sinew then dice into 1cm cubes. Refrigerate until required.

6 To fry oyster crackers, heat vegetable oil in a saucepan to 200°C. Carefully fry dehydrated oyster crackers, one at a time until puffed and crisp (10 seconds). Drain on paper towel and season to taste. Break into smaller pieces.

7 Strain beetroot juice mixture and season to taste. Add xanthan gum and blend with a hand-held blender.

8 Slice golden beetroots 2mm thick on a mandolin, then using a 2cm cutter, cut into rounds. You will need about 50 rounds. Mix ascorbic acid with cold water in a bowl and add yellow beetroot. Drain just before using. Peel and dice red beetroot.

9 To serve, dress the diced beef with the extra-virgin olive oil in a bowl and season to taste. Dress diced beetroot with the thickened beetroot juice and season to taste. Spread 2 tbsp (50gm) oyster cream onto each plate. Top half the cream with diced beetroot, avoiding adding too much beetroot juice. On the other side of the cream, place 5 discs of golden beetroot alternating with pieces of oyster cracker. Garnish with chive flowers and red garnet amaranth.

PREPARE AHEAD Oyster crackers, diced beetroot and yellow beetroot can be made a day ahead.

WINE MATCH 2016 Pizzini Nebbiolo, King Valley, Vic.

UNDER

BIG

SKIES

Leave the big smoke behind and embark on a wild adventure. Discover the majesty of Australia's Red Centre at Uluṟu-Kata Tjuṯa or immerse yourself in the outback at South Australia's Flinders Ranges or in the rugged Kimberley. Here, authentic Australian dishes put native ingredients front and centre.

Bullo River Station

Escape the big smoke and sample a taste of the outback with a stay
at this remote Northern Territory working cattle station.

Set on 500,000 acres of privately owned countryside at the convergence of the Bullo and Victoria Rivers, Bullo River Station is a working cattle station in the Northern Territory near the Western Australian border. The station's pristine landscape is carved with gorges and waterfalls, making it one of Australia's most breathtakingly beautiful stations.

Encircled by the coffee-coloured waters of the Victoria River and rugged hills inscribed with Aboriginal rock art, this vast property is not only home to around 3000 Brahman-cross cattle but also a variety of local fauna species including wallabies, dingoes, wild buffalo, native and migratory birds, fish and crocodiles.

In earlier years, outback hospitality was a lifeline for travellers, who would break a journey en route, stopping for several days to recover. With this spirit of outback hospitality, guests are invited to experience life on a working cattle station at Bullo.

Accommodation includes 12 contemporary guest rooms, designed by interior designer Sibella Court, each with its own king- or king-twin beds, air-conditioning and ensuite. Guests can help themselves to freshly baked treats or a drink with fellow travellers in the communal area. Wholesome meals and a drink at the end of the day will revive guests who have spent their time enjoying the station's many activities.

Owners Alex and Julian Burt's sustainable farming practices are in line with the Australian Wildlife Conservancy's approach. The Burts believe that cattle grazing and conservation projects can be managed in concert with the AWC.

Whether it's a day filled with dust, sweat and the exhilaration of station life or spent exploring waterfalls, swimming in remote waterholes, barramundi fishing and discovering Aboriginal rock art and wildlife, the Bullo River Station experience is unlike any other.

Guests are encouraged to roll up their sleeves and join the station team to do bore checks, lick runs, feed poddy calves and watch cattle mustering which usually takes place between May and September.

Birdwatchers will be entranced by more than 100 resident and migratory species on the property including emus, magpie geese, wedge-tailed eagles, brolgas and jabiru.

A short scenic helicopter flight is part of the all-inclusive rate as Bullo's half a million acres of breathtaking landscape must be seen from the air to be believed. Other activities include riding the station's stock horses along bush tracks and billabongs or tidal or freshwater fishing along the Bullo River with helifishing to remote locations an optional extra.

EXPLORE

• Dine around the campfire, under the silhouette of a Boab tree, as the sun sets over the Bullo River.

• Discover the resident and migratory birds that are attracted to Bullo's many waterholes and billabongs. Home to a diverse range of local wildlife, Bullo River Station is dedicated to the conservation of native species through its unique partnership with the Australian Wildlife Conservancy.

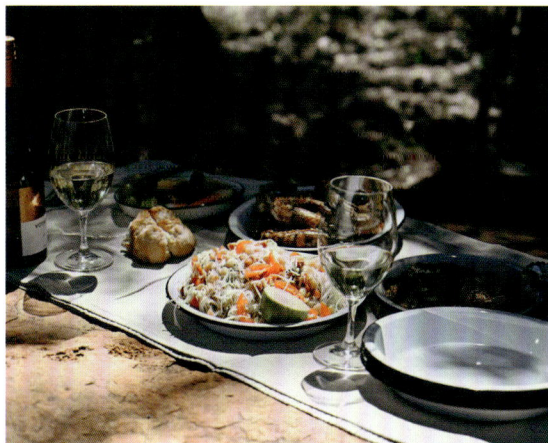

Red wine-braised beef with pale ale damper

SERVES 4 // PREP TIME 20 MINS // COOK 3 HRS 40 MINS

"A hearty stew and damper, cooked over an open fire, was a regular evening meal for drovers during a muster," says chef Jamie Carter. "This recipe honours that tradition, and is served under an ancient Boab tree at Bullo, as a tribute to those station workers."

2   bay leaves
6   thyme sprigs
6   rosemary sprigs
2½   tbsp extra-virgin olive oil, plus extra
     for drizzling
1   kg oyster blade, trimmed, cut
     into 5cm cubes
8   garlic cloves, finely chopped
1   onion, finely chopped
8   black peppercorns
1   tbsp tomato paste
750 ml bottle cabernet sauvignon or
     shiraz
300 ml beef stock
16   baby chat potatoes or other
     small potatoes
16   pickling onions, peeled
200 gm small Swiss brown mushrooms,
     quartered if large (see note)
1   bunch baby carrots, trimmed

     GRUYÈRE AND PALE ALE DAMPER
600 gm self-raising flour, sifted
80   gm coarsely grated Gruyère
325 ml pale ale
     Plain flour, for dusting
     Milk, for brushing

1 For Gruyère and pale ale damper, preheat oven to 220°C. Grease and line a large oven tray with baking paper. Place flour and cheese in a large bowl and make a well in the centre. Gradually add ale, and, using fingertips, combine to form a loose dough. Turn out onto a lightly floured work surface and knead lightly to bring together. Shape into an 18cm round. Using a sharp knife, score a 2cm-deep cross into the top. Brush top with milk and bake until golden and cooked (30 minutes).

2 Reduce oven to 150°C. Using kitchen string, tie bay, thyme and rosemary sprigs together to make a bouquet garni. Heat 1½ tbsp oil in a large heavy-based saucepan or casserole over high heat until almost smoking. Sear beef, in batches, turning until browned all over (8-10 minutes). Remove beef from pan and reduce heat to medium.

3 Add remaining 1 tbsp oil, garlic, onion and peppercorns and cook, stirring occasionally, until onion has softened (4-5 minutes). Stir in tomato paste until paste begins to catch on the base of the pan (1-2 minutes) then deglaze pan with wine. Increase heat to high and boil until wine is reduced by half (12 minutes). Add bouquet garni, stock, browned beef and remaining vegetables, except carrots, to pan and bring to a simmer. Skim off any impurities that rise to the surface. Cover with lid and braise for 1½ hours. Add carrots and cook, covered, for a further 30 minutes or until carrots are tender. Remove from oven and transfer vegetables with a slotted spoon to a bowl.

4 Transfer pan to the stovetop and simmer, uncovered, over medium heat until beef is very tender and sauce has thickened (30 minutes). Stir in vegetables and cook to warm through (8 minutes). Season to taste. To serve, divide braised beef and vegetables among plates with damper on the side.

NOTE For a decorative touch, "turn" a couple of the mushrooms in the braise. To do this, hold the tip of a paring knife in the centre of the mushroom cap and rock the blade down from the centre of the cap so the edge of the knife scores a groove in the mushroom all the way to the edge of the cap. Repeat five more times for a star shaped pattern in the mushroom.

PREPARE AHEAD Red wine braised beef can be made to the end of step 3 a day ahead.

WINE MATCH 2018 Voyager Estate The Modern Cabernet Sauvignon, Margaret River, WA.

Coconut and lime semifreddo with mango sorbet

SERVES 12 // PREP TIME 20 MINS (PLUS FREEZING) // COOK 15 MINS (PLUS COOLING, FREEZING)

"With fresh mango in abundance at Bullo, this refreshing dessert with fragrant lime leaves, is perfect to cool down after a day spent in the Territory sun," says Carter.

400 gm coconut milk
395 gm sweetened condensed milk
1 tbsp finely grated lime zest
375 ml thickened cream
40 gm shredded coconut, toasted
400 gm frozen chopped mango
80 gm icing sugar
3 lime leaves, centre vein removed, finely shredded
1½ tbsp lime juice, or to taste
30 gm raw macadamias, finely chopped
Boab nut shells (optional; see note) and pansies, to serve

1 Line base and sides of a 13cm x 25cm cake tin with baking paper, leaving a 5cm overhang around all sides. Prepare a large bowl of iced water.
2 Combine both milks in a saucepan and bring to the boil over high heat. Reduce heat to medium and simmer until thickened (15 minutes). Remove from heat and stir in lime zest, then place saucepan in bowl of iced water and stir mixture until cooled completely.
3 Place cream in a bowl of an electric mixer and whisk to stiff peaks. Fold cream into coconut mixture until just combined. Pour into prepared tin and sprinkle with toasted coconut, then freeze until set (4 hours or overnight).
4 Place frozen mango, icing sugar, lime leaves and lime juice in a high-speed blender and blend until smooth. Spoon mango sorbet over semifreddo, then freeze until set (4 hours or overnight).
5 To serve, using paper, lift semifreddo from tin. Using a hot knife, cut into slices and place in a boab nut shell or on a small plate. Sprinkle with macadamias and garnish with pansies. Serve immediately.

NOTE Boab nuts are produced by the boab tree, an Australian bush tree, which is easily identified by its swollen bulbous trunk with branches radiating from the top. Indigenous Australians have long used its shells as a canvas for creativity and storytelling, carving and painting them, while the boab fruit is considered highly nutritious and is ground into a powder.

PEPARE AHEAD You can make the recipe a day ahead.

WINE MATCH 2018 Voyager Estate Project Cane Cut Semillon, Margaret River, WA.

Arkaba

Take a walk on the wild side at this sheep station-turned-conservancy
set in South Australia's spectacular Flinders Ranges.

Located on the edge of Wilpena Pound, a spectacular geological amphitheatre in the Ikara-Flinders Ranges National Park, Arkaba offers one of the most exclusive wilderness experiences in Australia. With just five rooms on its 60,000 acres of outback ranges, and a guest to land ratio of one guest to 6000 acres, its luxury lies in the fact that only a handful of privileged guests share this experience.

About five hours' drive from Adelaide or just over an hour's private charter flight, Arkaba offers accommodation akin to staying with friends in the country – it is personal, down-to-earth and utterly immersive. No wi-fi access means that guests can truly unwind off-grid in the bush.

There are two ways to experience Arkaba. Guests can stay at the five-bedroom heritage Arkaba Homestead and explore the country on short walks or by safari vehicle in the company of field guides who'll share stories of the landscape to connect guests with the bush.

For those interested in a more immersive, sensory bush experience, explore the landscape on foot with The Arkaba Walk. On this three-night overland walking safari, guests stay in remote walking camps and sleep under the stars in swags to fully experience a sense of the scale of outback Australia underneath some of the clearest skies in the world.

The dining experience at Arkaba aims to connect guests to the landscape through exclusively South Australian produce and wines. Hosted by the manager or a guide, pre-dinner drinks around the campfire are followed by dinner at the camp table sharing stories with other guests.

For guests exploring Arkaba on foot, dinners are often enjoyed under the stars with three courses that taste even better in the distinctly Australian bush setting.

The experiences at Arkaba Homestead and the Arkaba Walk provide guests with the opportunity to learn about conservation challenges and see tourism dollars go into the protection of the landscape. It's hard to imagine that this private wildlife conservancy was once a sheep station. The removal of feral predators and grazers from the area has seen the happy reappearance of native mammals such as yellow-footed rock wallabies, brushtail possums and western quolls (the latter after an absence of more than 100 years).

Arkaba's backdrop, The Flinders, is one of the few places on the planet where you can walk through hundreds of millions of years of history. After all, this is where David Attenborough launched his series *First Life* as Ediacaran fossils in The Flinders provide evidence of the first traces of life on earth.

EXPLORE

• Head out for an evening wildlife drive to spot roaming emus and kangaroos. Finish with a ridge-top sundowner to drink in the endless outback views.

• Take a helicopter flight over the breathtaking ancient ramparts of Wilpena Pound and touch down at the Prairie Hotel for a beer at an authentic Aussie outback pub.

Roast beetroot tartlet with goat's feta and balsamic dressing

SERVES 4 // PREP TIME 30 MINS // COOK 40 MINS (PLUS COOLING)

"I make this recipe using local goat's cheese and produce for our vegetarian guests," says head chef Veronica Zahra. "It looks colourful and they appreciate the mix of earthy beetroot, sweet orange and the lactic tang of goat's cheese and ultra-crisp pastry disc."

500 gm small beetroot (about 5), peeled, cut into 2.5cm wedges
80 ml balsamic vinegar
160 ml orange juice
2 tbsp extra-virgin olive oil
2 tbsp caster sugar
3 sheets frozen puff pastry, defrosted (see note)
1 avocado, stone removed
1 tbsp lemon juice, or to taste
1 blood orange, segmented
120 gm goat's feta, crumbled
Baby sorrel, to serve

1 Preheat oven to 180°C. Place beetroot wedges in a roasting pan with balsamic vinegar, orange juice, oil and sugar, season to taste and toss to combine. Roast on the lower shelf of the oven until beetroot is tender and easily pierced with a knife (35-40 minutes). Set aside and cool slightly, reserving roasting juices.

2 Grease and line a large oven tray with baking paper. Stack 3 sheets of puff pastry directly on top of one another on a lightly floured surface. Roll out pastry until 3mm thick. Cut out four 15cm rounds from puff pastry and place on prepared tray and prick all over with a fork. Lay another sheet of baking paper over pastry rounds then place a second oven tray on top to weight the pastry down. Bake on the upper shelf of the oven with the beetroot until puff pastry is deep golden (35-40 minutes). Set aside until required.

3 Place avocado in a small bowl with lemon juice, season to taste and mash to combine. Set aside.

4 To serve, place a puff pastry round on each plate and spread avocado evenly over each. Divide beetroot among tartlets over avocado. Top with blood orange segments, feta and baby sorrel. Drizzle with roasting juices.

NOTE We prefer to use Carême puff pastry, which comes in pre-rolled 375gm sheets. If blood oranges are out of season, substitute navel oranges. Baby sorrel has an intense lemony tang that works well with the beetroot. If it's unavailable, substitute watercress or baby rocket.

PREPARE AHEAD Tartlet bases and beetroot can be made a day ahead.

WINE MATCH 2018 Voyager Estate The Modern Cabernet Sauvignon, Margaret River, WA.

Fried pastry cream with caramelised pear, vanilla and croquant

SERVES 6 // PREP TIME 30 MINS (PLUS REFRIGERATION) // COOK 50 MINS

"The fried pastry cream is an old Italian recipe traditionally served with game," says Zahra. "For my rendition, pillowy custard rounds are coated in polenta for crispness and served with caramelised pear, anglaise and croquant, which snaps in the mouth."

500	ml milk
5	egg yolks
55	gm caster sugar
2	tsp vanilla bean paste
90	gm plain flour, sifted
40	gm cornflour, sifted
55	gm instant polenta or panko crumbs
50	gm unsalted butter
250	ml grapeseed oil, for deep-frying
	White dianthus or other edible flowers, to garnish

VANILLA CRÈME ANGLAISE

125	ml milk
125	ml thickened cream
1	vanilla bean, split and seeds scraped
3	egg yolks
55	gm caster sugar

CROQUANT

125	ml water
110	gm caster sugar
90	gm flaked almonds, toasted

CARAMELISED PEARS

3	small beurre Bosc pears, peeled, halved and cored
110	gm white sugar

1 For fried pastry cream, grease and line base and sides of a deep 18cm square tin. Bring milk to a simmer in a large saucepan. Meanwhile, place egg yolks, sugar and vanilla bean paste in a large bowl, and using a whisk, stir to combine. Add flours and stir until just combined and smooth. While stirring continuously, gradually pour warm milk onto egg mixture until combined. Pour back into the pan and place over medium heat. Using a silicon spatula, cook, stirring continuously until mixture boils and thickens (1½ minutes). (The mixture will be thick and stiff, do not add extra liquid.) Spoon pastry cream into prepared tin, smooth top, cool slightly then cover the top directly with baking paper. Refrigerate until set (4 hours).

2 Meanwhile, for vanilla crème anglaise, place milk, cream, vanilla bean and seeds in a heavy-based saucepan over medium heat, and bring to a simmer. Meanwhile, place egg yolks and sugar in a large heatproof bowl and whisk until pale and thick (4 minutes). While whisking continuously, gradually add milk mixture until combined. Pour back into pan and place over low-medium heat. Using a silicon spatula, cook, stirring continuously until thickened (3 minutes). Do not boil. Strain through a fine sieve into a heatproof container. Cover the surface directly with plastic wrap to prevent a skin from forming. Refrigerate until chilled or until required. Makes 200ml.

3 For croquant, grease and line a large oven tray with baking paper. Place water and sugar in a saucepan, stir over low heat without boiling until sugar dissolves. Increase heat to high and simmer rapidly until a dark caramel forms (10 minutes). Working very quickly, stir in almonds until coated in caramel. Pour onto prepared tray and top with another piece of baking paper. Using a rolling pin, roll out mixture until very thin. Set aside to cool and harden. Once cool, break into desired pieces and store in an airtight container until required. This can also be frozen.

4 For caramelised pears, toss pear halves with sugar in a large bowl to coat. Heat a large non-stick frying pan over low-medium heat. Add pears and cook, turning and shaking the pan occasionally, until caramelised and cooked (10-12 minutes). (If pears begin to stick add a little water to release them from the base of the pan.) Set aside, covered, to keep warm until ready to serve.

5 To fry pastry cream, using a 7cm-round cutter, cut out 6 rounds from set pastry cream. Place polenta in a bowl. Add rounds, one at a time, turning to coat lightly in polenta. Place coated rounds on a tray lined with baking paper. Heat butter and oil in a small frying pan over medium heat and fry pastry rounds, in batches if necessary, turning halfway until light golden and heated through (2 minutes), then drain on paper towel.

6 To serve, place a fried pastry cream round on each plate, top with a caramelised pear and add a few croquant shards. Spoon a little crème anglaise onto plates and scatter with dianthus.

NOTE Croquant is a brittle made of nuts. When making it, ensure you have everything ready as the mixture will harden quickly making it difficult to roll. If necessary, place it in a hot oven for a couple of minutes to soften.

PREPARE AHEAD Pastry cream, vanilla crème anglaise and croquant can be made a day ahead.

WINE MATCH 2008 Moorilla Cloth Label Late Disgorged Sparkling, Berriedale, Tas.

One&Only
Wolgan Valley

Discover the natural beauty of the World Heritage-listed Greater Blue Mountains at this luxury resort with its authentically Australian menu, conservation-led activities and wildlife adventures.

Once you experience the unique blend of luxury, service and wildlife at Emirates One&Only Wolgan Valley's conservation-based resort in the World Heritage-listed Greater Blue Mountains, you'll understand why this is the perfect getaway.

Nestled in a private valley and protected by soaring bush escarpments, the 7000-acre resort is located between two national parks, Wollemi National Park and the Gardens of Stone National Park. Occupying just one per cent of the total land area, accommodation consists of 40 Australian Federation-style villas, each with separate living and bedroom areas, walk-in wardrobes, double-sided fireplace and private temperature-controlled indoor-outdoor pool. Wraparound verandahs allow guests to soak in the resort's wildlife reserve and spectacular views of Wolgan Valley and rugged 300-million-year-old sandstone escarpments.

The Main Homestead, with two dining destinations, bar and wine cellar, created by architects Turner + Associates and designer Chhada Siembieda, is an ode to its distinctly Australian surrounds, with timber and sandstone sourced within a 100-kilometre radius of the resort.

The Wolgan Dining Room, the resort's fine-diner, offers a garden-to-table philosophy with an authentically Australian menu based on regional produce. The menu changes according to the seasons and various ingredients are incorporated from the kitchen garden. Guests can enjoy private dining experiences, from romantic dinners under the stars to gourmet picnics. For a taste of the region, sip on the resort's locally distilled gin named for its 1832 heritage.

While environmental projects such as restoring Wolgan River and supporting wombat conservation are key to the resort, guests can participate in conservation activities to make a hands-on contribution to the restoration and protection of the reserve. The resort has a variety of native wildlife, dramatic landscapes and heritage that can be explored through a range of activities including wildlife safaris, nature walks, heritage tours, mountain biking and horse riding.

For those who prefer sports activities, there's a tennis court, 25-metre infinity pool, fitness centre, plunge pool, sauna and steam room. Stretch out in the wild on weekends with complimentary outdoor yoga sessions or rejuvenate with a pampering treatment at the One&Only Spa.

Emirates One&Only Wolgan Valley offers the rare opportunity to experience true luxury in a secluded haven in the Australian bush with award-winning regional dining and transformative wildlife experiences. This is Australia at its finest.

EXPLORE

• Sample a signature gin cocktail made with Wolgan's own blend. The 1832 Wolgan Gin provides a unique taste of Wolgan: distilled with purified water from Carne Creek that flows through the property and infused with seven hand-picked native Australian botanicals.

• Traverse Wolgan Valley's dramatic escarpments and walk under waterfalls on a guided hike to explore the nearby mystical Glow Worm Tunnel with its luminescent creatures.

Barramundi, native pepper and curry leaf butter

SERVES 8 // PREP TIME 20 MINS // COOK 30 MINS

"This dish can be done with large sesame leaves or paperbark," says executive chef James Viles. "For me, it's synonymous with camping trips where I use various wrappers and have the fish marinating during the day ready to cook on a barbecue or over coals."

8	barramundi fillets (150gm each), pin-boned
20	curry leaves, fried
100	gm sea blite (see note)
100	gm karkalla, blanched (see note)
16	large fig leaves (see note)

CURRY LEAF BUTTER

250	gm butter
1½	tbsp grapeseed oil
15	curry leaves
1	onion, finely chopped
2	garlic cloves, finely chopped
10	gm ground cumin
20	gm yellow mustard seeds
3	fresh pepperberry leaves (optional)
40	gm crème fraîche
60	ml lemon juice

1 For curry leaf butter, heat butter in a saucepan over high heat and cook until foaming and nut brown (2-3 minutes) and pour into a heatproof bowl. Heat oil in same pan over low-medium heat, add curry leaves, onion, garlic, cumin, mustard seeds and pepperberry leaves, if using, and cook, stirring often, until golden and fragrant (8 minutes). Transfer mixture to a high-speed blender and blend to a smooth purée. Add browned butter and crème fraîche and process until well combined. Add lemon juice and season to taste.

2 To cook barramundi, preheat oven to 180°C. Place fig leaves in pairs on two oven trays lined with baking paper, place a barramundi fillet, skin-side up, on top of each pair of leaves (alternatively if not using fig leaves place fish directly on baking paper). Coat with a small amount of curry leaf butter. Bring leaves up and around fish, securing with string if necessary. Roast fish until just cooked through (8 minutes). Untie, then using a blowtorch, brown the fish skin until crisp.

3 To serve, transfer fish on fig leaves to serving plates. Spoon warm curry leaf butter over each fish, then top to the side with fried curry leaves, sea blite and blanched karkalla.

NOTE Karkalla (also known as pigface and beach banana), and sea blite (also known as sea spray), are available from select greengrocers. If large fig leaves are unavailable, overlap smaller fig leaves.

WINE MATCH 2020 Brokenwood Stanleigh Park Vineyard Chardonnay, Hunter Valley, NSW.

Whipped bush honey, dried milk, macadamia and burnt honey custard

SERVES 8 // PREP TIME 15 MINS // COOK 35 MINS (PLUS COOLING, OVERNIGHT REFRIGERATION)

"The inspiration for this recipe came from an orchard in Bowral nine years ago, seeing my bees pollinating the trees next to a dairy with incredible milk," says Viles. "Over the years I've created various iterations of the classic marriage of milk and honey."

2 tbsp whipped honey (such as Malfroy's Gold or Wellington Apiary; see note)
60 gm freeze-dried honey
30 gm raw macadamia, shaved on a mandolin
Elderflowers and white linaria, to serve

BURNT HONEY CUSTARD
600 ml pouring cream
100 gm honey
7 eggs
Scraped seeds of 1 vanilla bean
Pinch of salt

DRIED MILK
40 gm liquid glucose
60 ml water
15 gm caster sugar
60 gm full-cream milk powder
Cooking oil spray

1 For burnt honey custard, preheat oven to 200°C fan-forced. Place cream in a saucepan and heat to 60°C. Remove from heat and whisk in honey until well combined. Whisk eggs in a large bowl until combined, then gradually pour over warmed cream mixture and whisk until combined.

2 Pour custard mixture into a 13cm x 21cm ceramic ovenproof dish. Bake custard on the top shelf of the oven until the top is a deep golden brown (20 minutes). (The custard will be slightly split on the base and a little wobbly in the centre; this is as it should be and it will come together again with blending.) Remove from the oven and set aside to cool. Leave the oven on.

3 Meanwhile, for dried milk, place ingredients in a small bowl. Using a hand-held whisk, combine until smooth. Lightly grease a non-stick 22cm-diameter frying pan with oil spray. Then wipe off the excess with paper towel. Place the pan over the lowest heat, pour in half the mixture and cook until mixture starts to evaporate and brown underneath and at the edges (3-4 minutes). Remove pan from heat, spray around the edges lightly with oil, stand for 1 minute, then carefully peel off the dried milk and place, pale-side up on an oven tray lined with baking paper. Wipe pan clean, then repeat with the remaining milk mixure. Place the tray with the dried milk in the oven and cook until the top is dry to the touch and lightly browned (4 minutes). Cool on the tray then transfer to an airtight container until required.

4 Transfer custard, scraped vanilla bean seeds and salt to a high-speed blender and blend until a smooth custard. Transfer burnt honey custard to a 500ml airtight container and refrigerate until chilled and set to a thick mousse-like custard.

5 To serve, place a small spoonful of whipped honey in each bowl and cover in honey custard. Top with shards of dried milk, freeze dried honey, shaved macadamia and elderflowers and white linaria.

NOTE Malfroy's Gold honey is available online at malfroysgold.com.au and Wellington Apiary honey is available at The Essential Ingredient and select delicatessens.

PREPARE AHEAD Burnt honey custard and dried milk can be made a day ahead.

WINE MATCH 2018 Tahbilk Cane Cut Marsanne, Nagambie Lakes, Vic.

Longitude 131°

A journey to the Red Centre is a revelatory experience at this luxury resort with its unparalleled views of Uluru, outback dining and deep spiritual connection to the ancient desert landscape.

The best place to witness the spectacle of Australia's Red Centre is at Longitude 131° with its views of World Heritage-listed Uluru and Kata Tjuta. It is a place to connect to the outback and its heritage and explore the unique beauty of the desert.

An unrivalled location that boasts one of Australia's most famous natural icons in its backyard, Longitude 131° is a unique experience that deserves its bucket-list status. Nestled among rust-red dunes, 16 tented pavilions, gathered in an arc as if around a campfire, elevate outback luxury to new heights. Each luxury tent features floor-to-ceiling windows to take in unparalleled Uluru views. Watch the magical changing lights of Uluru from the comfort of your bed, luxury swag or day bed on the balcony in the cool night air, complete with green-fuelled fireplace. The premium two-bedroom Dune Pavilion offers exclusive views of both Uluru and Kata Tjuta, local Indigenous artworks and separate living and sleeping areas. The wraparound deck reveals a dramatic plunge pool overlooking the vast desert frontier.

Longitude's kitchen creates dishes that showcase the best produce sourced from around the country; think Cape Grim beef from Tasmania, Murray River cod from Victoria and oysters from South Australia's Coffin Bay. Alongside this fine produce, the kitchen team incorporates many native bush ingredients as well as Indigenous cooking techniques in the daily changing menus, adding a local flavour and sense of place to the dining experience.

Rather than following Western seasons, Longitude's dining concept aligns itself with the local Anangu seasons, which identify with three of the region's strongest climate characteristics – the Kuli or "hot time", the Nyinnga or "cold time" and the Piriakutu, when the winds blow from the northwest and the food plants begin to flower. Dine overlooking the nation's spiritual heart of Uluru at the Dune House restaurant or under the stars at Table 131°, the lodge's exclusive outdoor dining event. The feeling of being in a natural theatre is heightened by the chefs who work by torchlight to present four sumptuous courses. Under starry night skies, the lodge guide regales guests with tales of the southerly constellations glowing brightly above.

Longitude 131° celebrates the sunburnt country in all its glory and offers a dining experience to match, bringing the best of the nation's produce to the centre. Artfully mixed with the flavours and stories of the land's ancient culture, guests are treated to a real taste of Australia.

EXPLORE

• Sleep under outback stars in a custom swag, sip on a nightcap, and enjoy uninterrupted views of the southern skies.

• The vibrant bloom of the honey grevillea is an important bush food for the local Anangu as well as sustaining a host of birds and insects. The flower nectar is prized as a bush dessert and blooms in spring.

Confit ocean trout, fennel, lemon myrtle, roasted almond, sea succulents

SERVES 4 // PREP TIME 10 MINS (PLUS STANDING) // COOK 30 MINS

"Ocean trout and fennel has always been a classic combination," says executive chef Ryan Ward. "At Longitude 131°, we add a light pickle to the fennel to cut through the richness of the trout and season the dish with fragrant lemon myrtle and salty ice plant."

1 baby fennel (120gm)
1 tbsp chardonnay vinegar
　Sea succulents such as karkalla, ice plant or samphire (see note), to serve

CONFIT OCEAN TROUT
4 ocean trout fillets (100gm each)
75 gm caster sugar
60 gm sea salt flakes
2 tsp lemon zest
1 litre olive oil

LEMON MYRTLE OIL
80 ml grapeseed oil
2 fresh or 5 dried lemon myrtle leaves (see note), crushed

ROASTED ALMOND MILK
75 gm slivered almonds
125 ml mineral water
　Almond oil, optional, to taste

1 To make cure for confit, place trout in a bowl. Combine sugar, salt flakes and lemon zest in a small bowl. Scatter curing mixture over fish and turn to coat. Cover and refrigerate for 30 minutes. Remove trout from curing mixture. Rinse thoroughly then pat trout dry with paper towel and stand at room temperature for 45 minutes.

2 Meanwhile, for pickled fennel, cut fennel in half and shave on a mandolin. Place shaved fennel in a bowl and toss with vinegar. Cover and refrigerate until required.

3 Meanwhile, for lemon myrtle oil, place grapeseed oil and lemon myrtle leaves in a small saucepan; heat oil to 80°C in a small saucepan over high heat. Remove pan from heat and stand until required, then strain and discard leaves. Makes 80ml.

4 For roasted almond milk, place slivered almonds in a dry pan, stir over low-medium heat until toasted (5 minutes). Transfer hot nuts to a high-speed blender. Add mineral water and blend until very smooth. Season to taste with salt and almond oil, if using. Makes 180ml.

5 For confit ocean trout, preheat oven to 50°C fan-forced. Meanwhile, heat oil to 50°C in a saucepan over high heat, using a thermometer to check the temperature. Arrange trout fillet in an oven dish to fit trout very snugly, then add hot oil to just cover. Bake for 8-10 minutes; the fish should remain pink throughout but be cooked enough so that you can cut it with a very sharp knife (because of the low temperature the fish will have a translucent appearance as the proteins have not been set). Set aside in oil.

6 To serve, warm almond milk in a small saucepan over low heat then place a spoonful to one side of wide shallow bowls. Remove trout from oil, pat dry on paper towel, then divide among bowls. Place half the fish over the almond milk with pickled fennel to the side. Drizzle fish and almond milk with lemon myrtle oil and top with sea succulents.

NOTE If sea succulents are unavailable reserve the fronds from the fennel and use these instead to garnish the trout. Salmon can also be used in this recipe. If lemon myrtle isn't available, substitute 2 tsp chopped fresh lemongrass.

PREPARE AHEAD Lemon myrtle oil and roasted almond milk can be made a day ahead.

WINE MATCH 2019 Brown Brothers Winemaker's Series Fiano, King Valley, Vic.

King prawns, smoked almond tarator, white soy, witlof and capers

SERVES 4 // PREP TIME 30 MINS (PLUS HEATING BBQ) // COOK 6 MINS

"Spencer Gulf prawns are sweet and rich, so you don't need a lot to make them delicious," says Ward. "The heat of the barbecue brings out the flavour of the shells. Dressed with brown butter and white soy, I recommend making double as they are moreish."

12	extra-large Spencer Gulf prawns (85gm each)
125	gm unsalted butter
2	tsp white soy sauce (shiro), or to taste (see note)
20	caperberries
2	small red witlof, leaves separated
20	small flat-leaf parsley leaves
	Lemon cheeks and sourdough bread, to serve

SMOKED ALMOND TARATOR

250	gm smoked almonds
5	confit garlic cloves (see note)
1	tbsp lemon juice
1	tbsp Sherry vinegar
2	tsp Dijon mustard
250	ml warm water
100	ml extra-virgin olive oil
100	ml vegetable or confit oil
	Smoked salt, to taste

1 For smoked almond tarator, blend almonds, garlic, lemon juice, vinegar, mustard and water in a high-speed blender until smooth. With motor operating, slowly pour in combined oils; blend until smooth and emulsified. Add more warm water if required to loosen to a thick mayonnaise consistency. Season generously with smoked sea salt. Makes 500ml. Refrigerate until required.

2 Bring a charcoal barbecue to high heat.

3 Meanwhile, using sharp scissors, cut the prawns from the top of the head to start of the tail lengthways on the underside to butterfly. Peel the body of the prawn, leaving the head and tail shell parts intact. Using a sharp knife, cut a slit along the back of the prawns and remove the digestive tract.

4 Heat butter in a small heavy-based saucepan over medium heat until butter foams and turns a nut brown (3 minutes). Remove the pan from the heat, cool slightly, then stir in the soy sauce, a little at a time until seasoned to taste.

5 Cook prawns, butterflied-side down first for 1 to 2 minutes, turn over and cook for a further minute or until just cooked through.

6 Divide prawns among plates, pour over the warm brown butter, white soy dressing and scatter with caperberries, witlof leaves and parsley. Serve with a generous spoonful of smoked almond tarator, lemon cheeks and sourdough.

NOTE Shiro or white soy sauce is a Japanese soy that's lighter in both appearance and flavour than its more common darker counterpart. To confit garlic, separate a bulb of garlic into cloves and peel. Place garlic in a small saucepan with a couple sprigs of thyme and a bay leaf, add enough olive oil to cover; cook over low heat until the garlic is tender but not browned (30 minutes). Cool and store garlic in oil. Reserve confit oil for tarator.

WINE MATCH 2016 Printhie Wines Super Duper Chardonnay, Orange, NSW.

El Questro Homestead

A visit to this luxury homestead perched on the clifftop in the vast and rugged Kimberley landscape promises a new frontier for immersive adventures with an authentic Australian appeal.

Nestled within the Kimberley's vast and ancient landscape and hidden among burnt-orange cliffs and lush, green lawns sits El Questro Homestead, a pocket of luxurious exclusivity from which to explore the 700,000 acres of magical surrounds that must be seen to be believed.

This 10-suite retreat perched on the clifftop with views over the tranquil Chamberlain River offers understated luxury accommodation for up to 20 guests. The premium Chamberlain Suite cantilevered over the Chamberlain Gorge offers panoramic views of the Kimberley with floor-to-ceiling windows and balcony. Perfect for couples, its indoor-outdoor double deluxe bath and alfresco dining area are designed to make the most of romantic sunset views. The Homestead Garden Rooms, Gorge View Rooms and freestanding Cliff Side Retreats each feature a king-size bed, ensuite, freestanding bath with Aesop bath products and private balcony.

Dining at El Questro Homestead is an extension of the Kimberley experience with menus inspired by the richness of the produce of the Ord River Valley. Enjoy breakfast on the veranda with uninterrupted views to the Chamberlain Gorge as the morning sun warms the surrounding ranges with a soft pink glow. Lunch is served at a communal dining table under a shady awning as guests swap tales of their adventures and enjoy a glass of Western Australian wine. Dinner sees local produce paired with the best wines from around the country. Guests can also choose to dine at the Homestead's private locations. The modern Australian menu changes daily and showcases local, seasonal produce.

Homestead guests are offered complimentary excursions to allow for a fully immersive Kimberley experience. With almost 700,000 acres of rugged ranges, gorges and waterfalls to explore, the Homestead's surrounding landscape is dramatic and expansive with something for everyone from adventurous explorers to novice hikers.

Complimentary tours include a cruise along the Chamberlain River, a four-wheel drive guided history, nature and wildlife tour, an early-morning birdwatching tour, an exclusive afternoon swim at Zebedee Thermal Springs, watching the sunset at Buddy's Point and guided walks to the Kimberley's spectacular gorges.

For an optional extra, take a Homestead helicopter tour to see El Questro from a different perspective or soar over lush rainforests and between cliffs before landing near remote waterholes and waterfalls to enjoy a swim and gourmet picnic. Whatever you choose, El Questro has something to satisfy all tastes and adventurers.

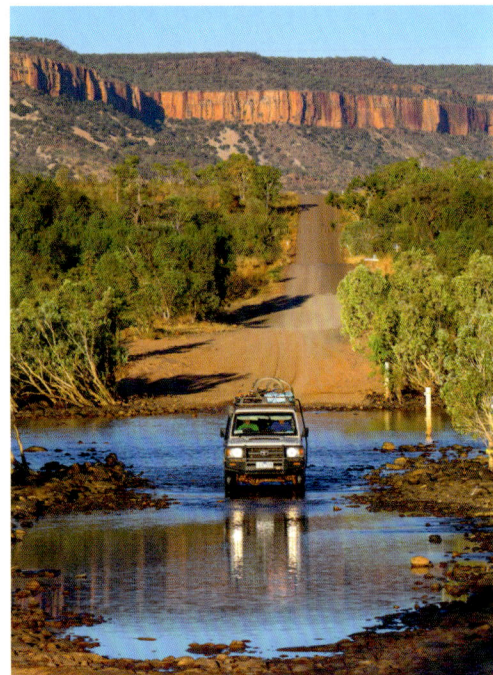

EXPLORE

• Take a helicopter flight to
a remote corner of El Questro to
visit spring-fed Miri Miri waterfall.
Cascading over a 50-metre drop,
Miri Miri is the perfect place for
a refreshing dip and picnic.

• Enjoy a romantic dinner under
the outback stars at a private
dining location overlooking
Chamberlain Gorge.

Harvey beef tenderloin with pumpkin purée, mushrooms, green asparagus and port wine jus

SERVES 4 // PREP TIME 45 MINS // COOK 7 HRS (PLUS REFRIGERATION)

"Supporting local producers such as Harvey Beef and its fine range of meat is important to us; here I showcase it with a silky pumpkin purée and use the bones for a rich port jus," says executive chef Matthias Beer.

2	tbsp extra-virgin olive oil, plus extra
1	garlic clove, bruised
2	fresh bay leaves, bruised
4	thyme sprigs, bruised
4	pieces beef tenderloin (200gm each)
350	gm asparagus, trimmed
100	gm Swiss brown mushrooms
40	gm butter
	Nasturtium leaves, to serve

PORT WINE JUS

1	kg chopped beef bones
1	tbsp vegetable oil
1	red onion, halved
1	large carrot, coarsely chopped
1	celery stalk, coarsely chopped
2	garlic cloves
30	gm tomato paste
1	thyme sprig
1	bay leaf
60	ml port wine

PUMPKIN PURÉE

300	gm peeled and diced butternut or Kent pumpkin
2	tbsp extra-virgin olive oil
2	garlic cloves, finely chopped
1	thyme sprig
30	gm butter

1 For beef stock for port wine jus, preheat oven to 200°C. Place beef bones in a roasting pan and roast until well browned (40 minutes). Heat 1 tbsp oil in a large saucepan over high heat, add onion, carrot, celery and garlic and cook, stirring until browned (8 minutes). Stir in tomato paste until darkened, then add 4 litres water, thyme and bay leaf. Bring to the boil, skimming off any impurities. Reduce heat to low and cook for 6 hours, topping up with water as necessary. Strain stock through a fine sieve, cool down quickly and refrigerate until chilled. Makes 1 litre.

2 For port wine jus, place port in a saucepan then carefully flambé. Remove the fat coagulates from top of beef stock then add the stock to the pan. Boil over high heat until reduced by three-quarters and syrupy (20 minutes). Makes 200ml port wine jus. Cool, then transfer to a container and refrigerate until required.

3 For pumpkin purée, preheat oven to 180°C. Toss pumpkin with oil, garlic and thyme in a small roasting pan. Roast until tender but without too much colour (25 minutes). Transfer to a blender and blend with butter until smooth, adding a little water if necessary to loosen. Season to taste. Transfer to an airtight container and refrigerate until required.

4 For beef, preheat oven to 200°C. Place olive oil, garlic, bay and thyme in a bowl. Add beef and bring to room temperature. Remove beef from oil mixture brushing off any herbs. Heat a large heavy-based ovenproof frying pan over high heat. Sear beef on both sides until well browned (6 minutes). Transfer the pan with the beef to the oven and cook for a futher 6 minutes for medium-rare. Set aside to rest (5 minutes).

5 Meanwhile, for asparagus, toss with extra oil then season to taste. Heat a large frying pan over high heat. Add asparagus; cook, turning frequently until tender (5 minutes).

6 For mushrooms, heat butter in a small frying pan over medium-high heat. Add mushrooms and season; cook, turning frequently until lightly browned (5 minutes).

7 To serve, reheat pumpkin purée and port wine jus in two small saucepans. Spoon a little pumpkin purée onto each plate. Carve each piece of tenderloin into three and place on the plate with asparagus and mushrooms. Spoon around a little port wine jus and garnish with nasturtium leaves.

PREPARE AHEAD Port wine jus and pumpkin purée can be prepared a day ahead.

WINE MATCH 2017 Dominique Portet Estate Cabernet Sauvignon, Yarra Valley, Vic.

Crisp-skinned red emperor with lemon myrtle risotto, heirloom tomatoes and prosecco jus

SERVES 4 // PREP TIME 25 MINS // COOK 1 HR

"There is huge excitement when I get to use a red emperor caught off the West Coast," says Beer. "The texture and taste of this fish is incredible combined with the creamy lemon myrtle risotto and prosecco jus – the perfect WA dish woven with native ingredients."

4	250gm red emperor fillets
	Sea salt flakes, to taste
2	tbsp extra-virgin olive oil
20	gm butter, chopped
	Nasturtium leaves, to serve

PROSECCO JUS

60	gm butter, chopped
1	golden shallot, thinly sliced
2	garlic cloves
1	thyme sprig
3	bay leaves
4	black peppercorns
200	ml prosecco
100	ml pouring cream
15	ml lemon juice

LEMON MYRTLE RISOTTO

600	ml vegetable stock
5	dried lemon myrtle leaves (see note)
30	ml extra-virgin olive oil
1	golden shallot, finely chopped
3	garlic cloves, finely chopped
200	gm arborio rice
70	ml dry white wine
	Zest of 1 lime
30	gm grated mature cheddar
20	grn butter, chopped

HEIRLOOM TOMATOES

400	gm heirloom tomatoes
2	tbsp coarsely chopped dill
2	tbsp extra-virgin olive oil

1 For prosecco jus, melt 40gm butter in a small heavy-based frying pan over medium heat and cook shallot, stirring until softening (3-4 minutes). Add garlic, thyme, bay leaves and peppercorns and cook, stirring until fragrant (1-2 minutes). Increase heat to high and add prosecco and flambé, cook until reduced by a third. Reduce heat to low, then whisk in cream until combined, followed by remaining butter and lemon juice, whisking continuously until incorporated. Strain through a fine sieve and season to taste.

2 For lemon myrtle risotto, place stock in a saucepan with lemon myrtle leaves and slowly bring to the boil. Reduce heat, cover and keep at a gentle simmer, remove lemon myrtle leaves. Heat oil in a wide saucepan over low-medium heat. Add shallot and garlic and stir occasionally until very soft (8-10 minutes). Add rice, stirring to coat and cook until just toasted (1 minute). Add wine, increase heat to medium and stir occasionally until wine is almost all absorbed (2-3 minutes). Add hot stock a ladleful at a time, stirring frequently, until stock is absorbed before adding more. Cook until rice is al dente (20-25 minutes), then remove from heat. Stir in lime zest, cheese and butter, then season to taste.

3 For red emperor, preheat oven to 200°C. Pat fish dry on paper towel and sprinkle with sea salt flakes. Heat olive oil in a frying pan over medium heat and cook fish, skin-side down until skin is crisp. Transfer pan to the oven and cook until fish is just cooked through (4 minutes).

4 Meanwhile, for heirloom tomatoes, slice tomatoes and place in a serving bowl, season to taste, then scatter with dill and drizzle with olive oil.

5 Remove the pan with the fish from the oven. Add butter to the pan, and once melted from the pan's heat, spoon over the flesh of the fish.

6 To serve, divide risotto among shallow bowls, placing it to one side then place fish, skin-side up over risotto. Place a spoonful of prosecco jus around the plate and garnish with nasturtium leaves. Serve with heirloom tomatoes to the side.

NOTE Dried lemon myrtle leaves are available online from native-food specialist stores.

WINE MATCH 2021 Gemtree Moonstone Savagnin, McLaren Vale, SA.

Spicers Peak Lodge

Experience the height of luxury at this lofty mountain retreat in Queensland's Scenic Rim with its elevated dining and wilderness setting.

Perched atop a plateau 1100 metres above sea level in Queensland's Scenic Rim with uninterrupted views of the Word Heritage-listed Main Range National Park, Spicers Peak Lodge offers one of Australia's most exclusive and lofty wilderness experiences. The lodge is the perfect retreat to immerse yourself in nature and marvel at the native fauna including koalas and wallabies.

Accommodation at this all-inclusive retreat includes a mix of luxury lodge suites, spa suites and loft suites in the main lodge, each with its own king-size bed, marble bathroom, complimentary minibar, fireplace or outdoor spa and mountain or rural views. Freestanding one- and two-bedroom private lodges perched on the escarpment are perfect for guests seeking more privacy with the luxury of a private outdoor infinity spa, double-sided fireplace and separate lounge and sleeping areas.

The lodge's fine-dining restaurant, The Peak, offers an ever-changing menu based on local, seasonal produce. A four-course lunch menu and tasting menu for dinner highlight "the best of Australia on a plate" ethos of the restaurant. Dishes include the likes of fresh pea tartlet, mascarpone and native pepper, Freestone sirloin, artichoke and beurre noisette and white chocolate, artichoke ice-cream and banana.

Blue Mountains squab and wagyu from Mayura Station in South Australia are just some examples of the produce that fits with The Peak's best of Australia theme.

The lodge runs a series of complimentary experiences for guests to enjoy. Try the Constellations by Campfire experience and stargaze as your guide takes you through the science of astronomy including history, navigation and constellations. Walk along one of the many self-guided tracks set in the 8000 acres of pristine wilderness, from a gentle walk around Lodge Plateau to the challenging mountain hike to Ryan's Lookout (poles required). Mountain bike tracks offer steep trails for daring guests. Go walkabout with a guided tour of the Lodge Plateau rim to learn about the history of Cedar Mountain from its humble potato farm origins to the luxury retreat of today. Explore the geology, ecology, flora and fauna of the area.

Culinary experiences extend beyond the restaurant. Picnic at the summit with 180-degree views of the Scenic Rim and a gourmet basket prepared by The Peak team with picnic rug, cushions, cutlery, glasses and drinks. And for the perfect way to unwind after all the day's activities, shake and mix your way through The Peak's cocktail or gin masterclasses or stroll to the top of the Lodge Plateau for a farewell drink and campfire canapé at sunset.

EXPLORE

• The remote, high altitude lodge, far from city lights, offers some serious stargazing opportunities. Sit around the campfire, drink in hand, to listen to ancient Aboriginal legends written in the twinkling night skies.

• Set on more than 8000 acres of wilderness, the lodge offers many scenic walks. Enjoy a picnic at one of the scenic lookouts complete with a picnic hamper prepared by the chefs, picnic rug and cushions to soak up the view.

9Dorf chicken with egg, mushrooms and saltbush

SERVES 4 // PREP TIME 35 MINS (PLUS COOLING) // COOK 10 HRS

"This dish showcases the amazing chicken and eggs from local producer 9Dorf Farms," says head chef Dean Alsford. "The addition of earthy mushrooms makes this a delicious, hearty meal." You will need to start this recipe a day ahead.

1.4	kg whole pasture-raised chicken
1	tbsp grapeseed oil
20	gm butter
4	pasture-raised eggs
1	bunch saltbush leaves, flash-fried, to serve

MUSHROOM DUXELLES

1	tbsp grapeseed oil
2	golden shallots (50gm), finely chopped
2	garlic cloves, crushed
2	tsp finely chopped rosemary
2	tsp finely chopped thyme
1	tsp sea salt flakes
80	gm unsalted butter, chopped
300	gm Swiss brown mushrooms, thinly sliced
160	gm portobello mushrooms, thinly sliced
50	gm shiitake mushrooms, thinly sliced

1 For chicken demi-glace, preheat oven to 240°C. Break down chicken into different cuts: Marylands, wings and the crown. Reserve chicken Marylands for another recipe. Being very careful not to tear the skin, remove the skin from the crown, by sliding your fingers gently along the flesh underneath it and reserve. Remove breasts from the crown. Retain the chicken frame. Reserve the breasts. Place the wings and frame on an oven tray and roast until browned (45 minutes). Transfer to a stock pot and add 3 litres cold water. Bring to the boil, skimming impurities off the surface. Reduce heat to a slow simmer and cook for 8 hours. Remove wings and frame, then strain stock into a large saucepan (you should have 1 litre), bring to the boil over high heat and reduce heat to medium and simmer until reduced to a demi-glace (15-20 minutes). Refrigerate until required. Makes 165ml.

2 For mushroom duxelles, heat oil in a large frying pan over medium heat. Add shallots, garlic, herbs and salt, and sauté, stirring until translucent (3-4 minutes). Add butter, when it is melted and starts to foam, add all mushrooms and cook, stirring frequently until golden and tender (6 minutes). Remove from heat and cool and strain off the excess butter. Using a stick blender (or food processor), pulse mushroom mixture until coarsely chopped. Refrigerate until required.

3 To prepare chicken breasts, roll plastic wrap out on a bench. Place chicken skin, outer-side down, over the plastic wrap, then place chicken breasts (top to tail) on top of each other on the skin. Roll into a ballotine, using the plastic wrap to wrap the skin around the chicken, then twist the ends of the plastic tightly to form a firm log shape then wrap tightly in foil. Place chicken in a saucepan of gently simmering water, then weigh down with a plate or smaller saucepan lid until chicken is cooked through and an internal temperature of 63°C is reached (25 minutes). Transfer chicken ballotine to a bowl of iced water to arrest cooking.

4 To serve, preheat oven to 200°C fan-forced. Unwrap the ballotine. Heat 2 tsp oil in an ovenproof frying pan over medium heat and cook, rotating until the skin is brown and crisp (5 minutes). Transfer pan to the oven and cook until heated through (5-10 minutes). Slice into 2cm thick portions.

5 Meanwhile, warm the mushroom duxelles and chicken demi-glace in separate small saucepans over low-medium heat. Heat remaining 2 tsp oil and the butter in a large non-stick frying pan over medium heat, crack eggs into the pan and cook gently until whites are set and the yolks are still runny.

6 To serve, spoon approximately ¼ cup warmed duxelles onto each plate, top with 2 slices of chicken then place an egg beside the chicken, spoon over the demi-glace and garnish with saltbush leaves.

NOTE In Australia saltbush typically refers to an edible blue-grey shrub, but there are about 60 species in this country alone; grey saltbush, a coastal variety with slender leaves, and old man saltbush, an inland plant with flatter, wider leaves, are the most commonly eaten.

PREPARE AHEAD Chicken demi-glace and ballotine can be made a day ahead.

WINE MATCH 2019 Vasse Felix Heytesbury Chardonnay, Margaret River, WA.

Marron with fermented and confit tomato

SERVES 4 AS AN ENTRÉE // PREP TIME 1 HR 15 MINS (PLUS FERMENTING, FREEZING, DRAINING)) // COOK 30 MINS

"This is the best of Australia on a plate with marron being one of the most premium seafoods available," says Alsford. "The tail is served with tomatoes from our onsite garden." You will need to ferment the tomatoes 1-3 weeks ahead.

2	**kg ripe, imperfect tomatoes (see note)**
60	**gm salt**
1	**gm xanthan gum**
12	**heirloom cherry tomatoes**
300	**ml olive oil**
1	**bunch dill**
300	**ml grapeseed oil**
4	**live whole marron (150gm each) (see note)**
	Chilli oil (optional), chive flowers and nasturtium leaves, to serve

1 For fermented tomatoes, one week in advance, chop tomatoes and toss with salt. Place in a glass container, seal and leave at room temperature for 1-3 weeks to ferment. Tomatoes are fermented when there is a rush of gas when the lid is removed and signs of bubbling, they will also have a fermented smell and taste. Blend fermented tomatoes in a blender until smooth, then place in a container and freeze (4 hours or overnight).

2 Line a sieve with cheesecloth and place over a bowl. Place frozen fermented tomatoes in a sieve over a bowl and leave to thaw without applying any pressure (20 minutes). (The clarified tomato juice will be colourless but flavoursome.) Blend clarified tomato juice in a blender with xanthan gum to thicken it. Place in an airtight container and refrigerate until required.

3 For confit tomatoes, heat oven to 130°C. Using a small paring knife, remove the tomato "eye" and score the base. Plunge into boiling water for 10 seconds then refresh in iced water. Using a knife, gently remove the skins to retain shape. Place cherry tomatoes and olive oil onto a small oven tray, cover and place in oven to until tomatoes are soft but still have bite (10 minutes). Place in fridge to cool.

4 For dill oil, blend dill and oil in a Thermomix on full speed at 60°C for 6 minutes. (Alternatively heat oil to 60°C then blend in a blender with dill.) Pass through a sieve lined with cheesecloth, discard solids. Transfer oil to a sealed glass jar and refrigerate until required.

5 Place marrons in freezer for 10 minutes to slow down metabolism. Working with one at a time, using a clean tea towel, hold the body flat to keep marron still, insert a sharp large knife into the base of the head to kill humanely. Next, with a twisting motion, remove the marron tails from the heads.

6 Cook marron tails in boiling water for 3 minutes and immediately plunge into a bowl of iced water. Once cooled, remove shell and digestive tract. Store in airtight container in fridge until required. Retain the shells and heads for stock.

7 To serve, slice each marron into 3 pieces and place back together in the centre of a bowl. Lightly season with sea salt flakes. Place three confit cherry tomatoes next to marron. Add enough fermented tomato water to reach a quarter of the way up the marron. Dress with droplets of dill oil. Garnish with chive flowers and nasturtium leaves and a few droplets of chilli oil.

NOTE Many greengrocers sell "imperfect" produce, a misnomer, as there is nothing wrong with the flavour; it simply means the produce has grown as nature intended and may not be uniform. Live marron are available from specialist seafood suppliers and may be stored in a breathable plastic container in the refrigerator for up to 3 days. If they're unavailable, substitute small lobsters.

PREPARE AHEAD Fermented tomatoes, dill oil and confit tomatoes can be prepared a day ahead.

WINE MATCH 2021 Seppeltsfield Grenache Rosé, Barossa, SA.

IN THE
VINES

An escape to one of Australia's wine regions is an epicurean delight with top-shelf pours and fine dining focused on local, seasonal produce. Wander through age-old vineyards in South Australia's Barossa Valley, sip at cellar doors in the Adelaide Hills, discover a cool-climate vineyard in the Mornington Peninsula and taste the bounty of Margaret River's terroir and produce.

Jackalope

This Mornington Peninsula hotel lives up to its mythical namesake as it juxtaposes contemporary architecture, a vineyard setting and avant-garde art to create a whimsical interplay between the ideal and surreal.

Situated on a private vineyard in the heart of the Mornington Peninsula wine region, Jackalope promises an experience to remember. With a monolithic, jet-black exterior, the hotel stands in sharp contrast to the verdant rolling vines, this juxtaposition is a nod to the hotel's namesake, a mythical creature – part jackrabbit, part antelope – that exists only in folklore.

The hotel unifies art, design, dining and storytelling in the guest experience, creating a whimsical interplay between the ideal and the surreal. Guests can enjoy food and wine experiences at the hotel's restaurants, bar and cellar door.

Jackalope's 44 rooms and suites, finished in a restrained palette of white and grey, are fitted with floor-to-ceiling windows and private terraces. Select suites sport views over the 30-metre infinity pool and vines while inside, the option of deep-soak, Japanese baths, and complimentary mini bar, movies and popcorn, deliver the ultimate in-room reverie.

Two restaurants surprise with contrasting takes on farm-to-fork dining. Doot Doot Doot's tasting menu is staged in several parts with à la carte options for entrée, main and dessert, served with a supporting cast of snacks and sides. The kitchen merges classic techniques with curiosity, creating playful dishes that pay homage to hero ingredients. In a nod to Jackalope's design, the team seamlessly combines contemporary with country – its trademark farm-to-table style underpins produce-worshipping dishes that find flavour in the unexpected.

By contrast, Rare Hare is a food and wine affair with a devil-may-care air. It boasts communal indoor and outdoor dining overlooking the vines and Jackalope Hotel's striking silhouette. A handcrafted wood-fired oven takes pride of place in the dining space. Produce-driven dishes balance heat, acidity, depth of flavour and texture on each plate.

Since 1876, McCormick House has stood gracefully on this storied site. Reborn as the hotel's bar, Flaggerdoot, it stands as an enduring reminder of the history of this property. Its current incarnation delights in the process of distillation; an experimental spirit stirs the daring cocktail menu, serving a mix of classics and in-house creations. The space is an infusion of forms; classic herringbone floors and open fires warm the room, while edgy installations and an electric blue pool table create a sense of curated cool.

Planted in 1989, the 28-acre Willow Creek Vineyard produces pinot noir, chardonnay, cabernet, pinot gris and sauvignon blanc. Jackalope offers tasting experiences where, over a glass of wine and a wander through the vines, guests can delve into details of vintages past and uncover the visual story of alchemy that inspires the art and design of Jackalope.

GEODE

EXPLORE

• In the winter months, grab a seat around the fire pit and indulge in the marshmallow trolley while the sun sets over the vineyard.

• Take advantage of Jackalope's complimentary transfers in a chauffeured Lexus to enjoy a relaxed lunch at one of the many fine-diners in the region.

Peninsula honey and yoghurt

SERVES 6 // PREP TIME 3 HRS (PLUS REFRIGERATION, SETTING) // COOK 40 MINS (PLUS COOLING)

Alyssum or other white edible flower, to serve

YOGHURT PARFAIT
125 ml thickened cream
250 gm goat's milk yoghurt
3 titanium-strength gelatine leaves
100 ml elderflower cordial
50 ml water
14 gm eggwhite powder (see note)
100 ml buttermilk

HONEY CRISP
100 gm caster sugar
10 gm Peninsula honey
45 gm unsalted butter
15 gm caster sugar, extra
75 gm eggwhite (2½ eggwhites)
25 gm almond meal
30 gm plain flour

HONEY GELÉE
2 titanium-strength gelatine leaves
170 gm Peninsula honey
180 ml hot water

HONEYCOMB
Cooking oil spray
130 gm caster sugar
100 gm liquid glucose
20 gm honey
20 ml water
6 gm bicarbonate of soda

MILK FOAM
250 ml milk
25 gm liquid glucose

LAVENDER SYRUP
50 gm coconut sugar
60 ml water
30 gm dried lavender

1 For yoghurt parfait, whisk cream to soft peaks, then fold into yoghurt. Refrigerate until required. Soak gelatine in a bowl of cold water until softened (3-5 minutes). Meanwhile, whisk cordial, water and eggwhite powder in a stand mixer on medium-high speed until doubled in volume (4 minutes). At the same time, warm buttermilk in a small saucepan over low heat. Squeeze excess water from gelatine, add to buttermilk and stir until gelatine is just melted without getting the mixture too hot or it will curdle. Slowly pour buttermilk mixture into mixer and continue whisking on medium speed until cooled (3 minutes). Fold buttermilk and eggwhite mixture into chilled cream mixture until combined. Transfer parfait to a 500ml container and refrigerate until set (3 hours) or until required.

2 For honey powder for honey crisp, line an oven tray with baking paper. Stir sugar, honey and butter in a small saucepan over low heat until sugar dissolves. Increase heat to medium and cook, without stirring, until mixture reaches 160°C. Pour onto prepared tray and leave to harden (1 hour). Break toffee into pieces and blend in a high-speed blender to a honey powder. Weigh 50gm honey powder and store remaining honey powder in a sealed jar for another use.

3 For honey crisp, preheat oven to 160°C (do not use the fan-forced setting). Place 50gm honey powder, extra sugar, eggwhites, almond meal and flour in a bowl, using a hand whisk, mix until smooth. Place a honeycomb silicon mould (if using) on an oven tray lined with baking paper. (If you do not have mould, spread thinly into 6cm rounds on baking paper.) Using an offset spatula, spread batter over mould (or in rounds). Bake for 8 minutes. Working quickly, carefully remove from the mould, as the crisp will harden quickly (if spread on the oven tray, leave to cool on the tray). Repeat with remaining batter. Once cool, store crisp in an airtight container for up to 2 weeks.

4 For honey gelée, soak gelatine in a bowl of cold water until softened (3-5 minutes) then squeeze out excess water. Meanwhile, place honey in a small heavy-based saucepan and cook over medium heat until dark brown and caramelised (5 minutes). Taking care as the mixture will spit, gradually add hot water to honey. Remove from heat and add bloomed gelatine and stir until dissolved. Strain through a sieve into a 10cm square container. Refrigerate until set (1 hour) or until required.

5 For honeycomb, line a small oven tray with baking paper and spray paper with cooking oil spray. Stir sugar, glucose, honey and water in a deep saucepan over medium-high heat until dissolved, wiping down sides of pan with a wet pastry brush to prevent crystals forming. Boil until sugar syrup reaches 160°C (6-8 minutes). Remove from heat and whisk in bicarbonate of soda until dissolved (mixture will foam up). Working quickly, pour mixture onto prepared tray. Once cool, transfer to an airtight container to store until required. To serve, break honeycomb into small pieces.

6 For milk foam, preheat oven to 80°C. Place a wire rack over an oven tray and line rack with baking paper. Heat milk and glucose in a small saucepan to 85°C. Using a stick blender, blend with the head half in, and half out, of the milk to create foam. Using a spoon, skim foam and spread over the baking paper. Repeat twice more. Tilt the tray so any milk runs off from the foam. Bake milk foam until dry and crisp but without colour (3 hours). Cool, then store milk foam in the freezer until required.

7 For lavender syrup, stir sugar and water in a small saucepan over low heat until sugar dissolves. Increase heat to medium and bring to the boil. Remove from heat and add lavender and leave to steep and cool in the syrup. Strain syrup through a fine sieve and refrigerate for up to 2 weeks or until required.

8 To serve, evenly spoon yoghurt parfait among six bowls. Roughly break up the jelly with a spoon and place over the parfait. Lightly drizzle lavender syrup into the bowl. Crumble dehydrated milk foam and honeycomb into the bowl. Place honey crisp over the top. Garnish with edible white flowers such as alyssum.

NOTE Eggwhite powder is available from The Essential Ingredient. If it's unavailable, substitute 3 eggwhites and omit water.

PREPARE AHEAD All dessert components can be made a day ahead.

WINE MATCH NV Jacob's Creek Sparkling Moscato Rosé, SA.

Moreton Bay bug cooked in paperbark, lentils and native curry

SERVES 6 // PREP TIME 1 HR (PLUS OVERNIGHT SOAKING) // COOK 1 HR 15 MINS (PLUS INFUSING)

"The native bug curry is a true representation of the contemporary Australian concept that I base the dishes at Doot Doot Doot around," says executive chef Simon Tarlington. "It highlights unique Australian produce in an explorative yet approachable way."

Fried salt bush leaves and bronze fennel sprigs (see note), to serve

BRAISED LENTILS

300	gm Mount Zero green lentils, soaked
2	tbsp extra-virgin olive oil
5	golden shallots, finely chopped
3	garlic cloves, sliced thinly
125	ml red wine vinegar
2	bay leaves
1	tsp ground pepperberry (see note)
200	ml sweet dessert wine
1	sheet kombu, cut into 5cm squares, rinsed

NATIVE CURRY SAUCE

3	spring onions
4	cm piece ginger
4	garlic cloves
1	lemongrass stalk, white part only
2	long red chillies
¼	bunch coriander
2	tbsp grapeseed oil
¼	tsp each cumin, fennel and coriander seeds
½	tsp ground pepperberry
½	tsp ground turmeric
90	g finely grated palm sugar
200	ml coconut cream
500	ml coconut milk
100	gm macadamias, roasted
250	ml fish stock
8	each dried eucalyptus and lemon myrtle leaves (see note)
6	makrut lime leaves
	Anchovy fish sauce, to taste

MORETON BAY BUGS

50	cm paperbark (see note)
6	extra-large raw Moreton Bay bugs
20	gm finely grated palm sugar
2	tbsp extra-virgin olive oil
	Zest of 1 small orange

CARROTS

250	ml orange juice
1	star anise
90	gm unsalted butter
1	bunch baby carrots

1 For braised lentils, drain lentils and rinse under running water. Place lentils in a saucepan and add double the amount of water. Bring to the boil over high heat, reduce heat to medium, and cook until lentils are tender and hold their shape (5 minutes). Drain and spread over a tray, then refrigerate to cool (20 minutes).

2 Meanwhile, heat olive oil in a saucepan over medium heat. Add shallots and garlic and cook, stirring until translucent (3-5 minutes). Add vinegar, bay leaves and pepperberry and simmer until reduced by half (2-3 minutes). Add wine and kombu and simmer until reduced by half (4-5 minutes). Stir lentils into wine reduction and season with salt.

3 For native curry sauce, thinly slice spring onions, ginger, garlic, lemongrass, chillies and coriander (leaves, stems and roots). Heat oil in a heavy-based saucepan over low-medium heat. Add cumin, fennel and coriander seeds, pepperberry and turmeric and stir until fragrant (1-2 minutes). Add sliced ingredients and palm sugar, and cook, stirring occasionally, until lightly caramelised (5 minutes). Increase heat to high and add coconut cream and cook out (3 minutes). Add coconut milk, macadamias and fish stock and cook for flavours to develop (30 minutes).

4 Transfer hot sauce to a blender jug and blend until smooth. Add eucalyptus, lemon myrtle and lime leaves and set aside to infuse (1 hour). Strain sauce through a fine sieve and season to taste with anchovy fish sauce.

5 For Moreton Bay bugs, rinse and soak paperbark in cold water. Using a clean cloth in each hand, pull the tails off the bugs. Using a pair of sturdy kitchen scissors, cut down the inside of the tail shell on each underside and remove that section of shell. Gently ease out the tail meat and then remove the vein. Reserve the top hard shell. Refrigerate until required.

6 Preheat oven to 250°C. Combine palm sugar, olive oil and orange zest in a large bowl and season to taste with white pepper and salt. Add bug tails and turn to coat in seasoning. Return bug tails to reserved shells, opposite-side up. Cover each bug with a piece of baking paper cut to the same size as the bug tail. Drain paperbark, pat dry with paper towel, and cut bark into six pieces large enough to wrap around each shell. Secure paperbark around bugs with string.

7 Bake bugs until just cooked through (7 minutes), then rest in a warm place for 3 minutes before unwrapping.

8 Meanwhile, for carrots, combine ingredients, except carrots, in a small saucepan, and bring to the boil over high heat. Reduce heat to medium and cook for 5 minutes. Strain orange juice mixture through a fine sieve into a clean small saucepan. Thinly slice carrots on a mandolin. Add carrots to the saucepan and return to the boil, then remove from heat and stand (1 minute). Drain, discarding orange juice mixture.

9 Place a spoonful of lentils in the centre of six shallow serving bowls and a ladleful of native curry sauce. Top with carrots, a sliced bug, fried salt bush leaves and bronze fennel sprigs.

NOTE Pepperberry, dried eucalyptus and lemon myrtle leaves, and paperbark are available online from native-food specialist stores. Salt bush and bronze fennel are available from select greengrocers.

PREPARE AHEAD You will need to soak the lentils the night before.

WINE MATCH 2019 Willow Creek Vineyard Chardonnay, Mornington Peninsula, Vic.

The Louise

A luxury culinary retreat in South Australia's Barossa Valley offers a food and wine lover's paradise with local, seasonal produce, cellar-door tastings and a restaurant with its own kitchen garden.

Located in the heart of South Australia's wine country, The Louise, with its 15 luxury suites nestled in Barossa's undulating vineyards, provides a gourmand's culinary retreat. Guests can relax in the sauna, soak in their private spa tub, enjoy a drink toasting the sunset, gaze across the vineyards from the infinity-edge lap pool, and enjoy pampering wellness treatments in absolute comfort.

Home to some of the best food and wine in the country, the Barossa is the perfect place for gourmet travellers to experience the abundance of the region. With food that creatively reflects a sense of place, the restaurants' kitchen teams are dedicated storytellers of the Barossa region, its produce and its people.

Two restaurants offer season-driven menus with a strong focus on the region, with 85 per cent of produce coming from the Barossa and South Australia. Appellation is The Louise's elegant fine-diner. Dinner at Appellation is a seasonally inspired set four-course tasting menu created from produce from its kitchen garden and local growers. The sommelier enhances the experience with a wine pairing for each course.

Embracing ancient food traditions, nothing is wasted at Appellation; whole beasts are broken down for meat and charcuterie and fruit and vegetables from the garden are preserved to be used throughout the year.

Three75 Bar & Kitchen offers bar snacks or a simple dinner with a list of classics such as wagyu burgers, prawn toasts, steak and frites, truffle fries and doughnuts and Jersey cream for something sweet. With sweeping views over the valley, it's an easy spot to catch the sunset and enjoy a casual snack and cocktail.

Guests can choose from a range of activities designed to make the most of their stay. Float over gnarled, ancestor vines in a hot-air balloon, enjoy a sunrise picnic breakfast with kangaroos in native bushland or tour the valley in a vintage car. Sip and taste your way through the Barossa's cellar doors, explore beautiful vistas and vineyards by bike or track and enjoy lunch at one of the Seppeltsfield wineries.

The Louise's bespoke Barossa Wellness experiences led by wellness coaches cover everything from relaxation and nutrition to exercise and pampering. Guests can add a private yoga session, wellness workshop or relaxation massage to their itinerary for the ultimate reboot.

A stay at The Louise is about creating the space to indulge, unwind and connect to a remarkable culinary culture. The Louise is the perfect place to slow down and take in the natural beauty and bounty of the Barossa.

EXPLORE

• Visit the Barossa Farmers Market on Saturday mornings for a food lover's paradise. Arrive early to spot local chefs gathering their produce for the week ahead. Grab a coffee and a pastry and don't forget to take a bag to carry the swag of local, seasonal produce on offer.

• Take a sunrise hike at Kaiserstuhl Conservation Park, just a short drive from The Louise, to spot local kangaroos, echidna and birdlife in bushland surrounds.

Poached rhubarb, smoked sheep's milk sorbet and native pepperberry

SERVES 6 // PREP TIME 1 HR (PLUS FREEZING) // COOK 1 HR (PLUS COOLING)

"Rhubarb and pepper is a classic combination but native pepperberry in the meringue elevates this to another level," says executive chef Kyle Johns. "It's paired with smoked sheep's milk yoghurt sorbet for a cooling effect." Start this recipe a day ahead.

SMOKED SHEEP'S MILK SORBET
500 gm sheep's milk yoghurt
150 gm caster sugar
100 gm liquid glucose
200 gm water
 20 gm lemon juice

POACHED RHUBARB
500 gm rhubarb stalks (1 bunch)
 80 gm ginger, thinly sliced
1.5 litres water
750 gm caster sugar

PEPPERBERRY MERINGUE
 3 eggwhites
200 gm caster sugar
 ½ tsp ground native pepperberry
(see note)

1 For smoked yoghurt, place half the yoghurt in a wide metal tray, place the tray in a larger deep tray to one side, on the other side, place another small metal container with the wood chips. Place a piece of hot charcoal on top of the chips, allow smoke to rise and then immediately cover the larger tray completely with foil and leave to cold smoke (30 minutes). The top of the yoghurt will turn a light brown from the smoke.

2 Meanwhile, for sugar syrup, combine sugar, glucose and water in a small saucepan over low heat and cook, stirring without boiling, until sugar dissolves. Bring to the boil for 1 minute. Remove from the heat and stir in lemon juice. Cool.

3 Combine the sugar syrup, the smoked yoghurt, and remaining unsmoked yoghurt in a bowl, then churn in an ice-cream machine. Transfer to an airtight container and freeze until required.

4 Trim rhubarb stalks, then scrape using a small paring knife (reserve peel). Cut rhubarb into 2cm pieces (reserve trimmings). Place rhubarb peel and trimmings in a large saucepan with ginger, water and sugar. Stir over low heat without boiling until sugar dissolves, then boil over medium-high heat until syrup is reduced by half (25 minutes). Strain into a clean saucepan.

5 Add rhubarb to the ginger syrup and cook over low heat until rhubarb is tender but still holds its shape (5 minutes). Place rhubarb pieces in a container and refrigerate until chilled or until required.

6 For pepperberry meringue, preheat oven to 100°C fan-forced and line 3 oven trays with baking paper. Whisk eggwhites in a bowl with an electric mixer until soft peaks form, gradually add sugar, whisking until stiff peaks form and sugar dissolves (8 minutes). Add ground pepperberry and whisk briefly to incorporate. Spread meringue very thinly over the prepared trays. Bake until meringue snaps when bent (1½ hours). Cool, then store in an airtight container until required.

7 To serve, spoon smoked yoghurt sorbet into chilled bowls. Using the back of a spoon, create an indent in the sorbet for the rhubarb. Spoon in rhubarb with some of the ginger syrup. Break off large shards of the pepperberry meringue and place around the sorbet and rhubarb. Serve immediately.

NOTE Native pepperberry is available from herbies.com.au and select delicatessens.

PREPARE AHEAD Smoked yoghurt sorbet, pepperberry meringue and poached rhubarb can all be made up to 2 days ahead.

WINE MATCH 2016 Swift Blanc de Noirs, Orange, NSW.

Blackened carrots, harissa, ricotta and za'atar

SERVES 4 // PREP TIME 30 MINS (PLUS SPROUTING) // COOK 1 HR 20 MINS

"The carrots here are cooked low and slow over fire, concentrating their sweetness and building a good char on the skin, and paired with harissa and za'atar," says Johns. You will need to sprout the lentils for this recipe three days ahead.

130 gm brown lentils (see note)
8 carrots (1.3kg)
Extra-virgin olive oil, for brushing
400 gm soft fresh ricotta
1 tbsp finely chopped chives
Micro coriander, to serve

HERB OIL
1 bunch spring onions, tops only
1 bunch parsley, leaves picked
1 bunch chives
200 ml grapeseed oil

HARISSA
1 red capsicum
100 gm golden shallots, halved
10 garlic cloves
2 long red chillies
250 ml extra-virgin olive oil
2 tsp cumin seeds
2 tsp coriander seeds
1 tbsp smoked paprika
1½ tbsp red wine vinegar

ZA'ATAR
1½ tbsp dried oregano
1 tbsp ground sumac
1 tbsp sesame seeds
2 tsp dried thyme
1 tbsp ground cumin
1 tbsp ground coriander
½ tsp fine sea salt

1 For sprouted lentils, soak lentils in filtered water overnight. The next day, drain and spread over a damp clean tea towel on a tray, cover with another damp towel or paper towel and set aside in a cool place for 2-3 days, keeping the towels damp by spritzing them with water.

2 For herb oil, coarsely chop onion tops and herbs and add to a blender jug. Heat oil in a small saucepan to 90°C; add to the blender jug. Blend on high until the oil is a vibrant green (3-5 minutes). Strain through a coffee filter or very fine sieve (1 hour) without applying any pressure. Refrigerate until required or for up to 2 weeks. Makes 100ml.

3 For harissa, preheat a charcoal or gas barbecue. Char-grill capsicum, rotating until blackened and blistered (20-25 minutes) and set aside loosely covered. Once cool enough to handle remove skins and seeds. Char-grill shallots, garlic and chillies, rotating until shallots and garlic are browned and chilli skins are blackened (6 minutes for garlic, 8-10 minutes for shallots and chillies).

4 Transfer garlic, shallots and chilli to a small frying pan and add olive oil and spices. Cook over a low heat, stirring frequently, until spices darken and smell fragrant (6 minutes). Transfer chilli mixture to a blender with capsicum and vinegar and blend until a smooth paste. Season to taste then transfer to a jar and refrigerate until required. Harissa will keep for up to 2 months. Makes 600ml.

5 For za'atar, combine ingredients in a small frying pan over low-medium heat and dry-roast until fragrant (3 minutes). Cool. Store in a jar until required. Za'atar will keep for up to 2 months. Makes ⅓ cup.

6 For carrots, heat a gas or charcoal barbecue to the lowest setting. Brush carrots with oil, season to taste, and grill over the barbecue, turning frequently, until all sides are charred and the thickest part of the carrot is cooked but still firm (25 minutes). Cooking like this will caramelise the natural sugars and concentrate the flavour of the carrots. Transfer carrots to a preheated 180°C oven if still hard. Keep warm until ready to serve.

7 To serve, place 2 tbsp ricotta on each plate. Using the back of a spoon, create an indent and spread the ricotta. Spoon harissa into the indents around the ricotta. Cut carrots into slices on an angle, keeping the carrot together to maintain the shape, then place on top of the harissa and ricotta. Drizzle carrot with herb oil and sprinkle generously with za'atar. Combine sprouted lentils, chives and micro coriander, and scatter over the carrots.

NOTE If you don't have a barbecue, char the carrots in a char-grill pan and finish cooking them in the oven. For lentils, if preferred, you can use a store-bought mixture of sprouted lentils and beans.

PREPARE AHEAD Herb oil, za'atar and harissa can all be made a day ahead.

WINE MATCH 2020 Gemtree SBE Grenache, McLaren Vale, SA.

Cape Lodge

This idyllic vineyard hotel in the Margaret River region is a drawcard for epicureans with its award-winning lakeside restaurant that highlights the best of Western Australia's bounty.

A stay at Cape Lodge – the Margaret River region's luxury vineyard hotel – is an epicurean's dream come true. The 22-room property, located on a 40-acre estate of manicured gardens, bushland, lakes and vineyards, offers an idyllic hideaway. Nestled in the spectacular beauty of Australia's South West, Cape Lodge is the ultimate escape for those in search of relaxation and culinary delights.

The lakeside Cape Lodge restaurant offers guests a daily changing dinner menu showcasing the best of the region's produce. Highlights include marron tortellini, one of many dishes on the menu that shows off the Western Australian delicacy. Other local produce that regularly appears on the menu includes black truffle foraged from Manjimup or nearby Cowaramup.

The kitchen's menu has a strong focus on fresh, local ingredients of uncompromising quality. The Margaret River region is abundant with fresh produce – free-range beef and lamb, sustainable seafood, marron from local dams and locally produced cheese and organic vegetables.

Dinner in the restaurant is available as a chef's tasting menu. A dynamic local wine list, including a cellar collection of back vintages from some of Margaret River's best producers, as well as the estate's own wines made exclusively for Cape Lodge from its 23-year-old vineyards, ensures a good pour. Guests can enjoy a tour and tasting in the vineyard to discover a little about what makes these wines so special.

Cape Lodge is perfectly placed in the heart of wine country with some of the most celebrated producers and restaurants just a stone's throw away. The comfortable new Cape Lodge guest vehicle awaits to whisk guests off for more wining and dining further afield.

During the cooler months, Cape Lodge takes advantage of the winter black truffle season with truffle hunts, long lunches and truffle masterclasses.

Guests looking for a culinary experience that draws on the rich bounty of the Margaret River can book in for a class at The Cape Lodge Epicurean Experiences & Cooking School. Building on the success of Cape Lodge's cooking demonstrations and hands-on classes, this calendar of epicurean experiences, tours and masterclasses shines the spotlight on South-Western produce and local producers, winemakers, farmers and chefs. Whether it's a visit to a traditional-method chocolate producer or olive grove and oil factory, or a masterclass in local free-range pig butchery or sausage-making, Cape Lodge's experiences will suit all tastes.

EXPLORE

• Take a dip or snorkel in "the Aquarium" before breakfast – stroll down a goat track through fragrant peppermint trees to a magical natural swimming hole, protected from the surf by granite rocks.

• Head to Moses Rock, a secret beach spot adjacent to Cape Lodge, with a bottle of Champagne and sunset picnic hamper to toast the sun as it sinks into the Indian Ocean.

Grilled Pemberton marron, Parisian gnocchi, leek and fish chowder

SERVES 4-6 // PREP TIME 30 MINS (PLUS FREEZING) // COOK 1 HR (PLUS REFRIGERATION)

"We are spoilt with fresh marron sourced straight off the boat of local fishermen," says executive chef Tony Howell. "Here, I pair Pemberton marron with fluffy Parisian gnocchi made from choux pastry and a decadent chowder."

4-6   live Pemberton marron (140gm each) (see note)
40   gm butter, melted
40   gm butter, extra
    Marigold petals, bronze fennel and lemon basil, to serve

FISH CHOWDER
200   gm butter
1   leek, thinly sliced
2   potatoes, peeled and chopped
1.5   litres fish stock
500   ml pouring cream

PARISIAN GNOCCHI
250   ml milk
30   gm unsalted butter, chopped
60   gm plain flour
2   tbsp finely chopped flat-leaf parsley
1   tbsp Dijon mustard
3   eggs

1 For fish chowder, melt butter in a saucepan over low-medium heat, add leek and cook, stirring until soft (5-8 minutes). Add potato and fish stock and bring to the boil. Reduce heat to a gentle simmer and cook until potato is tender (20 minutes). Transfer to a blender with the cream and blend until smooth, then pass through a fine sieve. Refrigerate until required. Reheat gently before serving.

2 For Parisian gnocchi, bring milk and butter to a simmer in a saucepan over medium heat. Reduce heat to low, add flour and beat continuously with a wooden spoon until a smooth dough forms and pulls away from side of pan (1-2 minutes). Transfer to a heatproof bowl, add parsley and mustard and stir until combined. Add eggs one at a time, beating continuously until incorporated. Transfer mixture to a piping bag with a 2cm plain nozzle.

3 To cook Parisian gnocchi, bring a large saucepan of salted water to the boil over high heat, pipe pastry into boiling water, cutting with a small sharp knife at 2cm intervals while piping to make gnocchi-shaped pieces. Cook in batches until gnocchi float to the top (1-2 minutes), remove with a slotted spoon. Drain well, place on a tray lined with baking paper, cool, cover with plastic wrap and refrigerate for 30 minutes.

4 Place marrons in freezer for 10 minutes to slow down metabolism. Working with one at a time, using a clean tea towel, hold the body flat to keep marron still and insert a sharp large knife into the base of the head, halving the head. Turn marron around and cut the body in half, then place cut-side up onto an oven tray.

5 Preheat grill to high, season marron to taste and brush with melted butter. Cook marron under the grill until just cooked through (5 minutes).

6 Meanwhile, heat extra butter in a large frying pan over medium heat and cook gnocchi, in batches, if necessary, turning until golden brown (2-3 minutes). Drain on paper towel.

7 To serve, divide gnocchi among bowls, then spoon around warm chowder and top with marron. Garnish with marigold petals, bronze fennel and lemon basil.

NOTE Pemberton marron are available from specialist seafood suppliers and may be stored in a breathable plastic container in the refrigerator for up to 3 days. If they're unavailable, substitute small lobsters. Marigolds, bronze fennel and lemon basil are available from select greengrocers.

PREPARE AHEAD Fish chowder and Parisian gnocchi can be made a day ahead.

WINE MATCH 2014 Tahbilk Museum Release Marsanne, Nagambie Lakes, Vic.

Rottnest Island tuna with blood orange salsa

SERVES 4 // PREP TIME 30 MINS (PLUS REFRIGERATION)

"This light spring dish goes hand in hand with the best time of year for tuna, blood oranges and locally made goat's cheese," says Howell. "Serve this as an entrée or a shared plate."

520 gm sashimi-grade tuna, cut into 1cm dice
Baby green and purple mustard leaves (mizuna) and extra-virgin olive oil, to serve

GOAT'S CHEESE CRÈME FRAÎCHE
100 gm fresh goat's cheese
100 gm crème fraîche
Lime juice, to taste

BLOOD ORANGE SALSA
2 blood oranges
50 ml extra-virgin olive oil
50 ml grapeseed oil
1 makrut lime leaf, centre vein removed, thinly sliced
1 tsp baby capers
½ tsp finely chopped dill
½ tsp finely chopped chives

FENNEL SALAD
1 baby fennel (150gm), trimmed, shaved on a mandolin
1 tbsp dill sprigs
1 tbsp finely chopped chIves

1 For goat's cheese crème fraîche, combine ingredients in a small bowl, season to taste, then refrigerate to regain thickness (1 hour) or until required.

2 For blood orange salsa, peel oranges with a sharp knife, then segment over a bowl to catch juice, and squeeze juice from remaining membranes. Cut each segment into thirds and reserve. Whisk both oils into the blood orange juice and season to taste. Add remaining ingredients and reserved chopped blood orange and stir to combine.

3 For fennel salad, mix ingredients together in a bowl. Add a splash of the salsa juices, season to taste and toss to combine.

4 To serve, divide fennel salad among plates, top with tuna then blood orange salsa, a pinch of sea salt, and two spoonfuls of goat's cheese crème fraîche. Scatter with baby mustard leaves and drizzle with olive oil.

PREPARE AHEAD Goat's cheese crème fraîche can be made a day ahead.

WINE MATCH 2021 Penfolds Bin 51 Riesling, Eden Valley, SA.

Sequoia Lodge

With elevated views over Piccadilly Valley, a stay at this luxury lodge at Mount Lofty is the perfect place to discover its unique food and wine, wellness, nature and history experiences.

Sequoia Lodge sits on the side of Mount Lofty, perched high above the Piccadilly Valley in the Adelaide Hills, a region currently being considered for UNESCO World Heritage status. The area's significance centres on its working agricultural (food and wine) landscapes, historic settlements, abundant wildlife, pure environment and continuing culture and practice.

Sequoia is named after the three giant Californian Redwood trees planted by original owner, Arthur Hardy, that remain on the property. Guests are greeted in a native garden with tall fescue lawns, bottlebrush, banksia, grevillea and African lillies and surrounded by native bushland.

Accommodation consists of 14 sustainably designed luxury suites with panoramic views over the majestic Piccadilly Valley. The retreat brings a new level of luxury to South Australia, with its intimate lounge area, immersive nature-inspired experiences, natural artesian spring-fed stone hot pools, infinity pool, day spa and valley rim campfire amphitheatre.

Sequoia connects guests with the stories of the region, its people and produce – from boutique to iconic. Led by a team of hosts experienced in local food and wine, wellness, nature and history, guests are taken on a journey of discovery.

Guests are introduced to the region with the Lodge Welcome, where each guest is invited to share the story that brought them to Sequioa, followed by campfire storytelling. Here the host shares the story of place starting from the original custodians of the land – the Kaurna people who shared the land with the neighbouring Peramangk people – to the present. Guests learn about the region's food, wine, wellness and nature offerings from powerful stories about the region's unique attributes.

Bespoke luxury experiences that celebrate South Australian stories – many not available to the public – are ready for guests to enjoy. Taste the abundant local produce at fine-diner, Hardy's Verandah Restaurant. Pamper and rejuvenate with wellness treatments. Take a guided walk through the bush, home to the world's largest surviving koala population. Hop on a private helicopter tour to take in the breathtaking views of the Adelaide Hills. Sip local drops with some of the region's leading vintners.

The kitchen team at Hardy's Verandah Restaurant takes guests on a culinary journey that incorporates the region's history and produce. Discover the restaurant's award-winning Asian-fusion style in the four-course Short Story à la carte menu or the seven-course Long Story dégustation.

EXPLORE

• Pack your swimsuit – even if you think it's a little chilly – the estate's natural artesian spring-fed stone hot pools are a must-do that will reinvigorate your body and soul.

• Develop a nose for wine with Sequoia's sommelier-led Le Nez du Vin experience.

Wagyu brisket, Black Angus tenderloin, scallop and pearl onion

SERVES 8 // PREP TIME 45 MINS // COOK 10 HRS

"I created this Korean-inspired recipe based on a dish my mother used to make for family birthdays, which is fitting as many of our guests also celebrate their own special occasions," says head chef Jin Choi. You will need to start this recipe a day ahead.

1.5 kg wagyu brisket, point-end, marble score 9+
1 nashi pear, peeled
1 tbsp lemon juice
600 gm Black Angus tenderloin, at room temperature
 Grapeseed oil, for cooking
8 scallops, roe removed

SOY SAUCE BASE
1 litre soy sauce
250 ml rice malt syrup
250 ml mirin
500 gm brown sugar
3 red apples, sliced
3 onions, thinly sliced
5 garlic cloves
1 bunch spring onion, chopped
100 gm ginger, sliced
1 cinnamon quill
10 gm black peppercorns

PEARL ONION PICKLE
10 pearl onions, halved
30 gm honey
150 ml white wine vinegar
250 gm olive oil
2 thyme sprigs
2 tsp salt

1 For soy sauce base, place ingredients in a large saucepan and bring to the boil over medium heat, reduce heat to a simmer and cook for flavours to infuse (40 minutes), then strain into an ovenproof dish that will fit the brisket snuggly.

2 For braised brisket, remove fat from brisket. Heat a large frying pan over high heat then sear, turning on all sides until browned (6 minutes).

3 Preheat oven to 140°C. Add brisket to the soy sauce base in the dish (brisket will be completely immersed in liquid), then cover with a cartouche. Cover dish with foil then braise until brisket is very tender (8 hours). Remove brisket from the oven and cool in the liquid. Refrigerate until required.

4 For pearl onion pickle, fill a saucepan with water. Using a skewer or clamp, mount a digital thermometer to the side of the pan. Place the pan over medium heat until water reaches 75°C. Combine ingredients in a large zip-lock bag, pressing to remove air before sealing securely. Place bag in the water adjusting the heat as necessary to maintain a constant temperature of 75°C (25 minutes). Remove bag from water, cool, then refrigerate until required.

5 Peel and slice nashi pear into 1cm-thick rounds, then using a 2cm-round cutter, cut out rounds. Brush with lemon juice and refrigerate until required.

6 Remove brisket from braising liquid and strain liquid into a large saucepan. Bring to the boil then simmer over low-medium heat until reduced to a thin syrup consistency (25 minutes). Return brisket to reduced liquid to warm through.

7 Meanwhile, preheat oven to 220°C. Heat an ovenproof frying pan over medium-high heat. Brush tenderloin with oil and season to taste, then sear until browned all over (6 minutes). Transfer to the oven and cook until medium-rare, with an internal temperature of 55°C. Set aside to rest for 10 minutes.

8 Meanwhile, drain pickled onions and pat dry on paper towel. Heat a little oil in a frying pan over medium-high heat and sear scallops for 30 seconds each side and pickled onion, cut-side down, for 1 minute or until onions are lightly charred and scallops just cooked through.

9 To serve, cut brisket and tenderloin into thick pieces and place on a plate with a scallop, a halved pickled onion and some pieces of nashi pear. Separate another halved spring onion and scatter onion petals on the plate and drizzle with a little of the reduced cooking liquid.

WINE MATCH 2021 Seppeltsfield Nero d'Avola, Barossa, SA.

Spiced lamb saddle, carrot purée and Jerusalem artichoke

SERVES 6 // PREP TIME 1 HR (PLUS PICKLING) // COOK 1 HR (PLUS RESTING)

"The spice mix sweetens the lamb and works well with the earthiness of Jerusalem artichokes, while the pickled mustard seed adds a pleasant bite," says Choi. You will need to make the pickled mustard seed five days ahead.

1.5 kg lamb saddle, boned, leaving 5cm
    skirt on each side
1 tbsp grapeseed oil
250 ml chicken jus
    Deep-fried kale and parsnip chips
    (optional), to serve

PICKLED MUSTARD SEED
25 gm yellow mustard seeds
2 tbsp Moscatel wine vinegar (see note)
3 tsp caster sugar
2 tbsp water

LAMB SPICE
2 tsp cumin seeds
2 tsp coriander seeds
1 tsp salt
¼ cup picked thyme leaves,
    finely chopped

CARROT PURÉE
100 ml freshly squeezed orange juice
100 gm grapeseed oil, plus extra,
    for cooking
1 kg carrots, coarsely grated
1 tsp salt

JERUSALEM ARTICHOKE
500 ml water
50 ml lemon juice
50 ml extra-virgin olive oil
1 tsp salt
2 tsp thyme leaves
500 gm Jerusalem artichokes,
    peeled and halved

1 For pickled mustard seed, place mustard seeds in a small saucepan, add enough cold water to cover and bring to the boil, then drain. Repeat blanching four more times to remove the bitterness from the mustard seeds. Meanwhile, combine vinegar, sugar and water in another small saucepan over medium heat, stirring to dissolve sugar. Transfer pickling liquid to a jar and add mustard seeds. Cool, then seal and set aside for 5 days before using.

2 For lamb spice, place cumin and coriander seeds in a dry frying pan, stir over low heat until fragrant and toasted (3 minutes), then cool. Blend the toasted spices in a food processor until ground then combine with salt and thyme.

3 Place lamb saddle, fat-side down, on a chopping board and scatter over the lamb spice. Bring the sides up and roll into a big sausage shape then tie at 2cm intervals with kitchen string to secure.

4 Preheat oven to 200°C. Heat oil in a large frying pan over high heat and sear lamb, turning until browned all over (6 minutes). Transfer to a roasting pan and roast medium (35-40 minutes). Rest loosely covered for 20 minutes.

5 Meanwhile, for carrot purée, place orange juice and 2 tbsp extra oil in a wide deep frying pan over medium heat. Add carrot and cook, stirring frequently, until carrot starts to soften (5 minutes). Reduce heat to low-medium, cover with a cartouche and cook, stirring regularly, until carrot is very soft (15 minutes). Transfer carrot mixture to a high-speed blender, add oil and salt and blend to a purée. Keep warm until required.

6 For Jerusalem artichoke, place water, lemon juice, olive oil, salt and thyme in a saucepan, add artichokes, cover with a cartouche and bring to the boil over medium-high heat. Reduce heat to medium and cook until tender (30 minutes).

7 Drain artichokes and pat dry on paper towel. Heat oil in a frying pan over medium heat and brown artichokes on each side (2 minutes).

8 To serve, place a spoonful of purée on the base of the plate, drizzle with pickled mustard seed, then cut two slices of lamb and place on top with some artichokes. Top lamb with jus, then kale and parsnip chips, if using.

NOTE Moscatel wine vinegar, a bittersweet vinegar made from muscat grapes, is available from The Essential Ingredient and Simon Johnson.

PREPARE AHEAD Lamb spice and carrot purée can be made a day ahead.

WINE MATCH 2018 Feathertop Sangiovese, Alpine Valleys, Vic.

STUART RIGG

Owner and director, Southern Crossings Australia

With a travel career that has spanned continents and industry sectors, but always inextricably connected to Australia, it was almost certain that British-born Stuart Rigg would one day call this corner of the world home.

In 2001 Rigg established Southern Crossings' Sydney-based Australian operations. In the two decades since, he has successfully navigated various local and global challenges to secure Southern Crossings' place as one of Australia's leading luxury travel companies. He now leads a talented team that shares his passion for personalised travel that resonates and his commitment to the highest standards of service.

For Rigg and his team, it is not so much about which hotel or room to recommend (they'll take care of that without a hitch), their real talent is curating itineraries that will take you off the beaten track and keep you ahead of the pack. Rigg's connections – both within and beyond the travel industry – open doors that others can't and allow his team to tailor personalised experiences others haven't even dreamt of. Well-travelled and well-connected, Rigg understands the desires of discerning travellers, enabling him to deliver on the company's mission of "enriching and inspiring by creating extraordinary journeys".

It is Rigg's ability to make the seemingly impossible possible and access the inaccessible that have earned him a place on industry boards both in Australia and abroad, and on such coveted international travel lists as the Wendy Perrin WOW List, *Town & Country*'s list of travel gurus and Condé Nast's list of the world's leading travel specialists. Rigg has also been an active member of the Tourism Australia Food and Wine advisory panel alongside some of Australia's leading chefs and culinary identities.

southern-crossings.com

Acknowledgements

This book was inspired by Southern Crossings' 30-plus year history of sharing Australia's finest travel experiences with the most discerning travellers from around the globe; and witnessing how significantly our unique destinations' fabulous food and wine experiences have flavoured their travels.

Created with the finest fresh produce, curated by a collection of talented providores, chefs and sommeliers, and enjoyed in some of the most spectacular settings, Australia's food and wine experiences are truly world-class. It was our intention with this book to share some of Australia's most amazing travel experiences through the epicurean experiences they offer.

Our grateful thanks to all of the very special properties featured in these pages who not only inspired this book, but so generously opened their kitchens and shared their stories, and whose support helped make this book possible. We are also very grateful to Tourism Australia and Ultimate Winery Experiences Australia, without whose partnership this project would not have been possible.

A big thank you to the *Gourmet Traveller* team who have so beautifully brought our vision to life.

An enormous thanks to my fellow Southern Crossings directors and the entire Southern Crossings team, including the talented travel designers who passionately curate and share Australia's most rewarding food and travel experiences with a dedication that only comes from a genuine love of what they do, and for which I am very grateful every day.

And a huge and heartfelt thank you to my long-time collaborator, Bettina Kramer, without whose support and loyalty, this, and many projects, would simply not materialise.

Finally, thank you to you, the reader, the foodie, the discerning traveller – we hope you enjoy this book as much as we have enjoyed creating it.

Stuart Rigg

TOURISM AUSTRALIA is the Australian Government agency responsible for promoting Australia to the world as a destination for business and leisure travel. The organisation is active in around 15 key markets, where it aims to grow demand for destination tourism experiences by promoting the unique attributes which will entice people to visit. Tourism Australia's objectives are to influence and encourage international and domestic travel to Australia, foster a sustainable tourism industry, and develop economic benefits to Australia from tourism. Our vision is to make Australia the most desirable and memorable destination on earth because this underpins everything we do at Tourism Australia. *tourism.australia.com*

ULTIMATE WINERY EXPERIENCES AUSTRALIA is an exclusive group of premium award-wining wineries that reflects the passion and innovation that has made Australian winemakers famous world-wide. From Victoria's Mornington Peninsula to Western Australia's Margaret River, this curated collection offers immersive winery experiences based around world-class wines, warm and knowledgeable hospitality and culinary excellence. Go beyond the cellar door for exciting behind-the-scenes adventures that epitomise the personality of a winery and its surrounding region. Enjoy an impeccable dégustation and discover how the provenance of a region connects with the terroir of the wine, learn how to blend your own unique wine, or meet the winemaker and savour first-hand the rich diversity that our country's many wine regions have to offer. *ultimatewineryexperiences.com.au*

SOUTHERN CROSSINGS

TOURISM AUSTRALIA

ULTIMATE WINERY EXPERIENCES AUSTRALIA

GLOSSARY

agar agar a setting agent derived from seaweed; available from health-food shops.

applewood smoking chips apple wood produces a mild yet delicate smoke with a hint of sweetness.

baby amaranth leaves also known as pigweed. The colour changes from bright green to deep burgundy in warmer weather. Small leaves are used for garnish, while large leaves are eaten like spinach.

baby green and purple mustard leaves also known as mizuna, this salad green has a peppery, slightly bitter flavour. Substitute watercress.

baby nasturtium leaves and flowers an edible flower available in a range of hues. Both the leaf and flower have a similar peppery bite similar to a radish.

baby sorrel immature leaves of the sorrel plant with an intense lemon tang.

coconut
flakes dried unsweetened, unsalted flakes of dried coconut flesh.
sugar made from the nectar of coconut blossoms from coconut palms, with a caramel taste and crumb-like texture.
vinegar made from the sap of the flowers of coconut palms. The vinegar has a cloudy, white appearance and less acidity than some vinegars.

coral trout wild-caught fish with sweet bright white flesh found mainly near reefs over the continental shelf of the Australian coast. Substitute hapuku, red emperor or other firm white-fleshed fish.

cream
pouring also called pure or fresh cream. It has no additives and contains a minimum fat content of 35 per cent.
thickened (heavy) a whipping cream containing thickener. Minimum fat content of 35 per cent.

crème fraîche a French variation of sour cream, it has a velvety texture and slightly tangy, nutty flavour. It can boil without curdling and is used in sweet and savoury dishes.

curry leaves available fresh or dried and have a mild curry flavour; use them like bay leaves in cooking.

Davidson's plums available frozen from native ingredient stockists. Substitute European plums.

dried lavender culinary lavender, Lavanandula angustifolia English lavender is used mainly in sweet recipes but forms part of the classic French Herbs de Provence mix.

edamame shelled soybeans that are usually bought frozen. Available from Asian food stores and major supermarkets.

finger lime a type of tiny citrus native to Australia. Also known as a caviar lime.

fish sauce also called nam pla or nuoc nam; made from pulverised salted fermented fish, most often anchovies. Has a very pungent smell and strong taste, so use sparingly.

flour
"00" high-gluten content flour suitable for pasta- and bread-making, which require the gluten component of the flour to be worked in order to provide the necessary structure.
buckwheat despite its name, buckwheat is a pseudo cereal, neither from grass nor grain, and is unrelated to wheat. The ground flour is gluten-free with an earthy taste. Common uses are in soba noodles and blini pancakes.
plain (all-purpose) unbleached wheat flour is the best for baking: the gluten content ensures a strong dough, which produces a light result.
self-raising all-purpose plain or wholemeal flour with baking powder and salt added. Also called self-rising flour.
tapioca derived from the starchy vegetable cassava root; often used as an alternative to traditional wheat flours and starches.

French tarragon this is considered true tarragon with soft green-grey leaves, available during cooler months.

fried shallots thinly sliced shallots that have been fried until crisp; a staple garnish in Vietnamese cooking.

galangal also known as ka or lengkaus if fresh and laos if dried and powdered; a root similar to ginger in its use. It has a hot-sour ginger-citrusy flavour and is used in fish curries and soups.

ghee clarified butter with the milk solids removed; has a high smoking point so can be heated to a high temperature without burning. Used as a cooking medium in Indian recipes.

glucose syrup also known as liquid glucose. Made from wheat starch and used in jam and confectionery making.

gochujang a Korean chilli paste.

golden shallots also called French shallots or eschalots. Small and elongated with a brown skin, they grow in tight clusters similar to garlic.

grapeseed oil an oil with a high-burn point favoured by chefs due its neutral taste.

horseradish a vegetable with edible green leaves but mainly grown for its long, pungent white root.

Jerusalem artichokes neither from Jerusalem nor an artichoke, this crunchy brown-skinned tuber tastes a bit like a water chestnut and belongs to the sunflower family. Eat raw in salads or cooked like potatoes.

juniper berries dried berries of an evergreen tree, it is the main flavouring ingredient in gin.

karkalla also known as pigface and beach banana; a succulent found among sand dunes and on cliff faces around the Australian coastline. It has a fleshy texture and a light salty flavour.

katsuobushi dried bonito flakes.

kinako a type of roasted soybean flour used in Japanese desserts.

koji made from steamed rice treated with a mould called Aspergillus oryzae. It is used by the Japanese to make everything from soy sauce, sake, miso and mirin.

kombu a form of edible kelp widely used in Japanese cooking to make broths. It can also be pickled, eaten fresh and deep-fried.

kosher salt made from large coarse crystals, making it suitable for the koshering process. It is popular with chefs, who find the larger flake size easier to pick up.

lemon myrtle Australian native herb with a lemongrass flavour and lemon verbena aroma. Substitute lemongrass.

lemongrass also known as takrai, serai or serah. A tall, clumping, lemon-smelling and -tasting, sharp-edged aromatic tropical grass; the white lower part of the stem is used in many Southeast Asian dishes.

makrut lime leaf sold fresh, dried or frozen, it looks like two glossy dark green leaves joined end to end, forming a rounded hourglass shape. A strip of fresh lime peel may be substituted for each makrut lime leaf.

marron a type of crayfish from Western Australia. Substitute lobster or scampi.

mirin a Japanese champagne-coloured cooking wine made of glutinous rice and alcohol.

Moreton Bay bugs have broad, flat bodies and a large carapace. Sometimes referred to as slipper or flat lobster, however unlike lobster they have no claws. Substitute lobster, scampi or large prawns.

moscatel wine vinegar made from muscatel grapes in Spain; sweet and aromatic with overtones of stone fruit, blossoms and honey.

paperbark harvested from paperbark trees; adds a smoky flavour to fish, chicken and vegetables.

pepperberry more versatile than peppercorns and used in both sweet and savoury dishes. The leaves, stems and berries have an aromatic peppery taste.

pickled ginger pink or red coloured pickled paper-thin shavings of ginger in a mixture of vinegar, sugar and natural colouring; used in Japanese cooking.

polenta also known as cornmeal; a flour-like cereal made of dried corn (maize). Also the dish made from it.

radicchio Italian in origin; a member of the chicory family. The dark burgundy leaves, which have a strong bitter flavour, can be cooked or eaten raw in salads.

rice malt syrup a thick, sweet-tasting syrup made from brown rice flour; a popular vegan substitute for honey.

rice vermicelli also known as sen mee, mei fun or bee hoon. Used throughout Asia in spring rolls and cold salads; similar to bean threads, only longer and made with rice flour instead of mung bean starch.

sake made from fermented rice; is used for marinating, cooking and as part of dipping sauces. Substitute dry sherry, vermouth or brandy.

saltbush leaves an edible blue-grey shrub; the leaves are fleshy with a salty, herbal flavour and are very versatile. Can be used fresh in salads, tossed in stir-fries, or the dried leaves can be ground and substituted for salt.

sea blite a coastal plant that can be steamed, stir-fried or blanched. Complements seafood well.

shaoxing wine Chinese cooking wine; also called shao hsing or Chinese rice wine. Made from fermented rice, wheat, sugar and salt, with an alcohol content of 13.5 per cent. Substitute mirin or sherry.

shiitake mushrooms, fresh also known as Chinese black, forest or golden oak mushrooms; they have the earthiness and taste of wild mushrooms. Large and meaty, they can be used as a substitute for meat in some Asian vegetarian dishes.

shiro (white) miso fermented soybean paste. Generally, the darker the miso, the saltier the taste and denser the texture.

sugar
palm also called nam tan pip, jaggery, jawa or gula melaka; made from the sap of the sugar palm tree. Light brown to black in colour and usually sold in rock-hard cakes. Substitute brown sugar if unavailable.
panela raw, unrefined cane sugar from Colombia with a lightly sweet molasses taste and warm caramel undertones.

rapadura an unbleached and unrefined whole cane sugar that is higher in minerals and antioxidants than regular white sugar. It has a high molasses content, which gives it its characteristic caramel-like colour.

sumac a purple-red, astringent spice ground from berries growing on shrubs that flourish wild around the Mediterranean; adds a tart, lemony flavour to dips and dressings and goes well with barbecued meat.

tamari similar to but thicker than Japanese soy; very dark in colour with a distinctively mellow flavour. Good used as a dipping sauce or for basting.

titanium-strength gelatine leaves we use sheets that are 5 gm each.

verjuice the unfermented juice from unripe grapes.

Vietnamese mint not a mint at all but a pungent and peppery narrow-leafed member of the buckwheat family. A common ingredient in Thai dishes, such as soups, salads and stir-fries.

witlof also known as Belgian endive; related to and confused with chicory. It can be cooked as well as eaten raw.

xanthan gum derived from fermenting sugar with a form of bacteria; used as a multi-use stabiliser and thickener. It has no discernible taste and a pleasing mouthfeel.

yellow bean paste (hugan jiang or taucheo) a cooking paste made from fermented yellow soybeans. Despite the name, the colour is more light to dark brown, and the paste may contain flour.

yuzu juice believed to be a hybrid of sour mandarin and Ichang Papeda, a slow-growing tropical lemon, the fruit has a tart flavour similar to grapefruit but with mandarin overtones and a highly aromatic perfume. Sold bottled. Substitute grapefruit juice or lime juice.

Thai basil also known as horapa; different from holy basil and sweet basil in both look and taste, with smaller leaves and purplish stems. It has a slight aniseed taste and is one of the identifying flavours of Thai food.

COOK'S NOTES

Measures & equipment

- All cup and spoon measures are level and based on Australian metric measures.
- Eggs have an average weight of 59gm unless otherwise specified.
- Fruit and vegetables are washed, peeled and medium-sized unless specified.
- Oven temperatures are for conventional ovens and need to be adjusted for fan-forced ovens.
- Pans are medium-sized and heavy-based; cake tins are stainless steel, unless otherwise specified.

Cooking tips

- When seasoning food, we use sea salt and freshly ground pepper.
- To blanch an ingredient, cook it briefly in boiling water, then drain. To refresh, plunge in iced water, then drain.
- We recommend using free-range eggs, chicken and pork. We use female pork for preference.
- Makrut lime leaves are also known as kaffir lime leaves.
- Unless specified, neutral oil means any of grapeseed, canola, sunflower or vegetable oil.
- To dry-roast spices, cook them in a dry pan, stirring over medium-high heat until fragrant. Cooking time varies.
- Non-reactive bowls are made from glass, ceramic or plastic. Use them in preference to metal bowls when marinating to prevent the acid in marinades reacting with metal and imparting a metallic taste.
- RSPCA Australia's advice for killing crustaceans humanely is to render them insensible by placing them in the freezer (under 4°C) until the tail or outer mouth parts can be moved without resistance; crustaceans must then be killed quickly by cutting through the centreline of the head and thorax. For crabs, insert a knife into the head. This process destroys the nerve centres of the animal.
- All herbs are fresh, with leaves and tender stems used, unless specified.
- Eggwash is lightly beaten egg used for glazing or sealing.
- Sugar syrup is made of equal parts sugar and water, unless otherwise specified. Bring mixture to the boil to dissolve sugar, remove from heat and cool before use.
- Acidulated water is a mixture of water and lemon juice.
- To sterilise jars and lids, run them through the hot rinse cycle in a dishwasher, or wash them in hot soapy water, rinse well, place on a tray in a cold oven and heat at 120°C for 30 minutes.
- To blind bake, line a pastry-lined tart tin with baking paper, then fill it with weights (ceramic weights, rice and dried beans work best).
- To clarify butter, cook it over low heat until the fat and the milk solids separate. Strain off the clear butter and discard the milk solids. You will lose about 20 per cent of the volume in milk solids.
- To brine, bring 300 gm fine sea salt, 275 gm white sugar, 5 crushed juniper berries, coarsely crushed, 2 fresh bay leaves, 1 tsp black coarsely crushed peppercorns and 1.5 litres water to the boil in a large saucepan over high heat, stirring to dissolve, then set aside to cool completely. Place duck crown in a non-reactive container and pour over brine to completely cover. Cover and refrigerate overnight. Remove crown from brine (discard brine) and pat dry with paper towel.

INDEX

are media *books*

Published in 2021 by Are Media Books, Australia. Are Media Books is a division of Are Media Pty Ltd.

Editor Joanna Hunkin

Food Director Sophia Young

Creative Director Hannah Blackmore

Content Editor Suzanna Chriss

Senior Food Editor Dominic Smith

Project Coordinator Georgia Moore

Head of Operations David Scotto

Business Development Director
Joe Revill

Business Development Manager
Amanda Atkinson

A catalogue record for this
book is available from the
National Library of Australia.
ISBN 978-1-76122-048-7

FOOD PHOTOGRAPHY

Photographer William Meppem

Stylist Lucy Tweed

Photochefs
Jimmy Callaway, Ismat Awan

Recipe Testing
Olivia Andrews, Max Adey

Wine Matches Samantha Payne

TRAVEL PHOTOGRAPHY

Tourism Australia, Voyager Estate,
St Hugo

Photographers
Paul Bester, Cameron Bloom, Sharyn
Cairns, Julian Cebo, Aaron Citti, Nick
Cooper, Maxime Coquard, Duy Dash,
Jampal Dawa, Ellie Feiss, Melissa
Findley, D Huynh, Masaru Kitano snaK
Productions, CJ Maddock, Hiroshi
Matsui, Hayley Nedland, Kate Nutt
Photography, Reuben Nutt, Martine
Perret, Matt Munro, Dan Preston, Sean
Scott, Shot by Thom, Luke Tscharke,
Nick Wall AirSwing Media, Emily
Weaving, Sue Wright

Special thanks to Bistro Rex and
Lifestyle Charters who generously
hosted the Southern Crossings
photography shoots.

The publisher would like to thank
Devitt Meats for supplying all the
meat in this book.

DEVITT
WHOLESALE MEATS

Published by Are Media Books,
a division of Are Media Pty Limited,
54 Park St, Sydney; GPO Box 4088,
Sydney, NSW 2001, Australia
Phone +61 2 9282 8000
aremediabooks.com.au

Published in partnership with
Southern Crossings
southern-crossings.com

To order books
Phone 1300 322 007 (within Australia)
Or online at aremediabooks.com.au

Printed in China by
C&C Offset Printing Co., Ltd

FSC
MIX
Paper from
responsible sources
FSC® C008047

SOUTHERN
CROSSINGS